Organizing By
The Book

Devotional Ideas From
God's Word

Sandra Felton

Organizing By The Book

Published by Five Smooth Stones Communication,
5025 S.W. 114 Avenue,
Miami, Florida 33165.

Unless otherwise identified, all Scripture quotations are taken from the King James Version of the Bible.
Other Scripture quotations are from the following sources:

INTRODUCTION

Organizing: A Christian Approach

What's the Big Deal about Getting Organized?

Here's the big deal. We Christians can't afford to fumble on living out the life God has designed for us to live just because we can't get our organizational act together. For us organizing goes beyond cleaning, tidying, and being on time.

We've got several strong reasons to put organizing right at the top of our priority list.

We want to do our best for our families, helping our older members where necessary, making our spouses happy, and raising our children in the nurture of the Lord. We want and need order and beauty in our homes.

We want to work for the Lord in spreading the gospel in whatever way our talent takes us. You may have musical talent. Maybe you can work with the worship music team in your services and/or give lessons to future worship team members. You may head up Vacation Bible School or teach in it. You may take snacks to your small church group or just show up regularly at your Sunday school class. Maybe you are a part of your church outreach program. Or volunteer in the church office folding bulletins. Or fixing meals for the sick or bereaved. Or --- well, you know more ideas that fit your abilities and interests than I do.

Finally we want to obey God's command to show hospitality to meet the needs of others. We are told many times in the New Testament to show hospitality and to entertain others. Maybe you will have one friend over for coffee or tea once in a while. Or entertain a new couple in the church. Possibly you want to have a party for your church friends, maybe even mixing your church and non-churched friends together. Or, like the woman who built a room to entertain the prophet, you can have house guests.

Being disorganized can seriously hinder your living the abundant and productive life God has for you in all three of these areas --- and others.

Transforming the Housekeeping Mind

Determination is good. Planning is good. Reading how-to books is good. Getting others to help is a valuable idea. Buying storage products can be very helpful. But none of these is the key to living an organized, fruitful, satisfying life. Change must come from within. Jesus reminds us that we can't put new wine in old wineskins (leather pouches used for storage) because the old container will break and the wine will spill. Neither can we stuff new habits in old thought patterns and expect it to last. Only by having our minds enlightened and renewed by God's word will vibrant and enduring change come.

Our desire is to fulfill our designated purpose and the Bible tells us how. The Bible is God's revealed will concerning salvation, first to the individual and then spreading to the world. The Bible also contains many practical ways to live so that our lives will be "more abundant".

This book spotlights ideas from the Bible that impact on our homes and lives. As we weave those thoughts into our lives day after day, unproductive ways of thinking and behaving will fade and the bright colors of God's way will form the patterns of living that please Him, satisfy us, and maybe even give us a chance to impress our unsaved friends and acquaintances with what God can do. All of this glorifies God.

There is a deeper meaning in what we do. Somewhere sacred and seldom seen we may sense that our home is an altar on which we can offer the sacrifice of praise and that our efforts are part of priestly service. The vision of that knowledge may fade and the mundane may return. But the memory of that insight forever changes to some degree how we live.

A Personal Word

The Bible says that the older Christian women should be willing to share with the younger women what they have learned about how to live a productive and godly life God's way. Because my spirit whispers to me I am not yet there, I am reluctant to place myself in the ranks of the "older women". But the number of calendars I have discarded over the years tells me no one would be surprised to find me in that group.

I am also reluctant to take my place as a teacher of others in how life should be lived is because I feel I have faltered so much myself and left so many lessons unlearned.

However, there is one lesson I have learned well the hard way that I can share with those who have not discarded as many calendars as I have or walked as far down the troublesome path of life as I have.

The lesson is to do your best to live a sensibly organized life. This book is about that lesson --- organizing. Your accomplishments in every area of your all important life will be greater if you learn to manage well your time, your activities, and your house.

The Heart of the Matter

"Peter, lovest thou me more than these", Jesus asked. And as I view my surroundings I ask myself, "Do I love him more than these things?" Because they hinder my living out His Holy Spirit within me, I need to answer this question honestly. Then I need to act on the answer.

If following His agenda for my life is more important than following my own disordered and cluttered way of life, I have got to make serious changes in how I think and behave. Get rid of beloved stuff. Change careless habits. Drop "important" habits and obligations that keep me overcommitted. Real love for Him demands real behavior changes.

The answer from my heart is this, "Yes, Lord, you know I love you." followed by action. If your answer is the same, join me in a new way of life.

So let us agree together on this one thing. There's a great, big, wonderful life out there waiting for us. Let's live it His way for Him to the fullest.

1 *Do All for the Glory of God*

"So whether you eat or drink or whatever you do, do it all for the glory of God."

1 Corinthians 10:31 (NIV)

"Whatever you do" covers a lot of things. Lofty, "spiritual" things like prayer, sacrifice, or missionary work would surely be included. But in this passage Paul specifically points to more mundane examples of what he means like just plain eating and drinking. He is talking about what we do in everyday life that reflects Christ to others.

We glorify God in everyday activities. This includes how we function in our homes. We have a choice about whether the house is beautiful and orderly, or messy and unattractive; whether it is clean or grubby, neat or cluttered.

On a daily basis keeping our house for the glory of God means taking care of too much clutter lying around, cleaning jobs that are w-a-a-y overdue, bills and banking that may be in a shambles, our propensity for keeping too much stuff. What we don't want is a dwelling that is in no condition to glorify God. (Whoa! For you perfectionist cleaners don't get sidetracked onto a side road of fanatical cleaning, that wouldn't glorify God either.)

You've got to make your own judgment on how to work out glorifying God in housekeeping. How good is "good enough"? As long as you and your family are happy enough with the condition of the house, when you can do what you need to do with a certain amount of efficiency, and if you can entertain with a certain amount of ease, then you are doing what glorifies God.

This area takes spiritual wisdom and balance. Even if we feel spiritually free to keep a messy house, it would probably not be wise. Think and pray as to how what we do in our homes will be "beneficial" and "constructive" - in short - how we can glorify God there.

✂ *Apply to your life* ✂

Walk through your house and find the areas that do glorify God.

Choose to work on one area that needs to change to glorify God.

State in one sentence how your house can glorify God.

2 *Corner of the Housetop*

"It is better to dwell in a corner of the housetop, than with a brawling (or quarrelsome) woman in a wide house."

Proverbs 21:9 (NIV)

One thing is clear from this verse: the atmosphere of personal relationships in the home is more important than the condition of the house itself. Shouting, nagging, complaining and teasing fill a home with contention.

Being loving is often not easy and requires that we lean heavy on following God's words about what our attitudes and actions should be. Some of us need to work harder than others at maintaining a "meek and quiet spirit, which in the sight of God is of great price." (1 Peter 3:4)

This is an especially hard posture to maintain when the husband and/or kids are messy and clutter up the order of the house that you are trying to keep nice. Although it can be done without brawling or quarreling, it probably can't be done without conflict.

People who clutter the house come to the problem with a number of issues that need to be addressed. Some are:

- They don't see clutter as a problem and would rather live with it than work very hard at cleaning it up. They may have been raised that way or simply are not sensitive to how bad it looks or how difficult it is to live with.

- They have bad habits of getting things out and not returning them. Sometimes they haven't designed places to store items so they are forced to leave them out or stick them anywhere. In short, they really have never learned how to be orderly, even if they wanted to.

- They have small regard for how much this bothers you. You are embarrassed to have people come in. You feel you can't pick up after them as fast as they can leave things out, nor do you feel that it is fair that you should have to.

How can we deal with this problem without becoming "a brawling woman" that none of us wants to become?

- Equip them with knowledge of how to do a task and the space (container or places) to put things.

- Be resolute about your goals for your house. You should not be forced to live with the problems and stress caused by somebody else's mess. (Warning: don't become a perfectionist and super picky.)

- Communicate in a way that makes sense to them, hopefully in a loving way after a good

- meal when the atmosphere is good and good will is running high.

- Change your actions so that their messiness impacts them negatively so that they will feel that it is in their best interest to change. This requires some courage and thought. You may stop picking up and instead just scoop all the clutter into a box. The messy person may become upset with you for not continuing to pick up but your action helps him becomes aware of the real problem.

It takes a wise woman indeed to make necessary changes without slipping into the quarrelsome category. But it can be, indeed must be, done.

ଔ *Apply to your life* ଶ

Can you think of one change you can make in order to make your management of the house more peaceful?

3 *What Pleases the Lord?*

"Live as children of light ...and find out what pleases the Lord. Be very careful, then, how you live - not as unwise but as wise."

Ephesians 5:8, 15 (NIV)

Can the command be simpler? Find out what pleases the Lord and be careful to live that way.

This takes some thought. Would it please the Lord for me to do something different from what I am doing in the house?

Because he hasn't said so specifically, I don't presume to know for sure whether God cares if:

- ◆ I am late to appointments.

- ◆ My clothes are scattered around.

- ◆ I have to spend a lot of time looking for misplaced things.

- ◆ I procrastinate in sending out sympathy, get well, or birthday cards.

- ◆ The children's school papers are not signed and returned on time.

We can all guess that he does care. But one thing is certain. He tells us to live wisely so we can fulfill commands he has clearly given such as:

- ◆ Bear one another's burdens. (Don't make work for others. Help them instead.)

- Love not only in word but in deed. (Don't fail to actually DO something for others.)

- Take care of the needy. (Don't carelessly become the needy person that others need to take care of.)

- Let your good works be seen so that your Father will be glorified. (Be productive.)

If our disorganized behavior interferes with any of these, I think I am on solid ground saying that God would like us to be more organized so we can do more for him.

ೞ *Apply to your life* ຠ

Think about it. What three things can you do that will help you live as a child of light? Use the space below (or your journal) to list three things that you think you can do to please the Lord. Make them small ones so you can put them into practice today or tomorrow. Then do them consistently day by day. After those are cemented, add one or two more things.

In that way you will be building wise behavior that will please the Lord.

To help you get started on your list of new habits, think about the areas listed below and choose three things (possibly small ones) you can do to please the Lord that you are not doing now:

Cleaning

Organizing

Entertaining

Children

Husband

Work

Support of others

Other areas in your life

Present these new activities as offerings of praise.

Finish Up What You Started

"The best thing you can do right now is to finish what you started last year and not to let those good intentions grow stale."

2 Corinthians 8:11 (The Message)

Did you ever start a job and run out of steam before you completed it?

- Perhaps it was a little job like straightening a drawer.

- Maybe it is a middle-sized job like picking up the living room.

- Or possibly it was a bigger project such as redecorating the living room or remodeling a closet.

Whatever the project was, leaving it unfinished acted as a discouragement to you and your motivation to upgrade the organization in your life. If you leave the litter from the half finished project sitting out waiting for your return, the distress will increase.

The church in Corinth got excited about taking up an offering for some needy Christians in another area. Somewhere along the way, the steam went out of their project.

Did they lose interest? Did the person in charge get distracted and drop the ball? Did their vision grow dim with time?

We don't know for sure, but we know that these things happen to us. We may run out of money, somebody may not show up to help, we may get sick or find a more interesting project. Like a dress that moves out of fashion, what we started hangs untouched.

Paul urged the people in Corinth to focus again on finishing the job. He wrote, "But now finish doing it." (2 Corinthians 8:11 NASV) He continues by telling them that just as they had the desire to start it, they needed to find the desire to complete it. In the next verse he indicates that they don't need to do it perfectly. In today's parlance we would say, JUST DO IT, get that bad boy finished up.

Eugene Peterson renders it this way in The Message, "The best thing you can do right now is to finish what you started last year and not to let those good intentions grow stale. Your heart's been right all along. You've got what it takes to finish up, so go to it." (The Message, Navpress, 1993, p. 450)

❧ *Apply to your life* ☙

The only thing left for us to do is to identify the unfinished project we are going to tackle first and, as Paul said, "Go to it!"

Name one job in your life you need to complete.

What is the first step you can take?

When do you estimate you can finish it?

Do you need more supplies or help to finish it? If so, get them.

5 *Folded? Really?*

"He saw the strips of linen lying there, as well as the burial cloth that had been around Jesus' head. The cloth was folded up by itself, separate from the linen."

John 20:6b, 7 NIV

The finding of the empty tomb of Jesus is one of the most significant and sacred scenes in the entire Bible. Mary had just told John and Peter that the authorities had removed the body so they had run to check it out for themselves.

The body of Jesus had been wrapped with strips of linen cloth. It was the custom of the day. Under his chin and knotted at the top of his head had been tied a cloth generally used to keep the mouth of the deceased closed in a dignified way.

Peter who reached the tomb first, looked inside. As Mary had said, there was no body. But Peter did see the strips of cloth, perhaps just lying still wound but empty of the body. But -- most interesting to our focus -- John spotlights the head cloth. It had been folded and placed to the side.

We don't know exactly what happened in the cave behind that rock covered door. We do know the power of God moved to raise his sacrificed son from the dead, confirming that the work of salvation had been finished. Sinful man could now be reunited with a holy God through the work of Jesus.

How did it happen? Was there a burst of energy, light and sound when the body of Jesus was again infused with life? Or, when the time came, did his spirit quietly return to his body so that he rose quietly just as though getting out of bed?

Did he have to free himself from the binding strips of cloth or did he simply rise through them in the same way he later passed through a locked door?

We don't know the details, but one thing is very clear about what went on behind that rock. Somebody thought it was important to take the time to neatly fold that head cloth and place it to the side.

Perhaps no other verse in the Bible speaks so clearly about God's view of order. At that momentous time, someone stopped a moment to be neat. Perhaps Jesus folded it, perhaps the angels. Someone did not want to drop it on the floor or leave it mixed with the strips of cloth.

Often the phrase, "Neat and tidy" sounds cute and insignificant to us. What happened in that cave indicates it is significant to God... and should be to us as well.

෬ *Apply to your life* ෧

Think about it. Do you think that order is important to God? Do you think that you value order enough?

Are sheets and towels folded in your linen closet?

When you fold clean clothes think of how God values your work.

I Put Away Childish Things

"When I was a child, I spoke as a child, I understood as a child, I thought as a child; but when I became a man I put away childish things."

1 Corinthians 13:11

In the middle of this poetic portion about love of 1 Corinthians Chapter 13 we find this very prosaic but beautiful statement about growing up. The principal of my junior high school (perhaps in desperation, poor guy) used to read it regularly in assembly to his still very immature charges. Undoubtedly he hoped it would hasten our replacing foolish ways with more adult behavior.

And inevitably we did grow up and we left behind most of our childish things. But maturing is often an uneven thing. We may develop in many areas, yet leave some seriously behind. Responsible adults have the opportunity to look back from time to time at their own development and bring those underdeveloped parts into adulthood.

As we look around we notice some adults are still careless and messy in their affairs, driving their husbands, wives, and maybe bosses crazy. Their ability, and maybe their desire, to order their world aright has lagged behind in their move into adulthood. They have not stepped up to the plate and taken their places as part of the orderly household team.

Some were never trained in childhood and now must discipline themselves how to live a more orderly life. Others were trained but it didn't "take." Some got hooked on keeping too much stuff and are now unwilling to do the hard work of overcoming this addiction. Still others have never recognized that something as mundane as keeping life in order profoundly affects important areas of life.

- They still drop clothes and towels for others to pick up.

- They indulge their "collections" even when keeping them litters the house.

- They frustrate others to whom order and beauty are important, unmindful of the law of love and caring they are violating and unaware of how much it hurts others to be forced to live in chaos because of their careless behavior.

But it is not too late. Overcoming ingrained disorganization is not easy. But as responsible adults we accept the obligation to "put away childish things" and become an adult in that aspect of our lives as well.

◌ॐ *Apply to your life* ◌

What childhood "bad habits" do you still follow?

What steps can you take to stimulate maturity toward a more ordered life?

7   *Playing Jesus*

"All things are lawful unto me, but not all things are expedient; all things are lawful for me, but I will not be brought under the power of any."

1 Corinthians 6:12

Our church is well known for its Easter pageant that depicts the life of Jesus up through his crucifixion, resurrection and ascension. A member of our congregation named Jim, who happens coincidentally to be a carpenter as Jesus probably was, plays the part of Jesus from year to year. When he grows a beard and lets his hair become longer, he bears a striking resemblance to the traditional depictions of Jesus. He has a remarkable ministry because of his opportunity to play Jesus each year.

In order to do that Jim has to pay attention to his physical appearance. Because he is spotlighted hanging on a cross in the climactic scene of the play, he cannot indulge himself in something like getting a tattoo or gaining weight. It may not be wrong in and of itself to do either, but it would ruin the portrayal of that important event. In effect, it would disqualify him from that service.

Paul wrote to the Corinthians, "All things are lawful unto me, but not all things are expedient; all things are lawful for me, but I will not be brought under the power of any." (1 Corinthians 6:12)

In the areas of time use, organizing, cleaning, and many other areas of life that are insignificant in and of themselves, we need to make sure we do what is expedient (useful, wise, advantageous, beneficial, prudent) as we act out Jesus before the world.

Wasting time unwisely, being messy, and keeping too much, leaving things lying around so the house is too messy to function well in --- none of these things are unlawful in and of themselves. But they are not expedient. They do not move us forward in our service of God. In fact they may hinder us.

There is a wide variation of many perfectly lawful ways we live our lives. Some of us are casual, maybe too casual. Some are uptight, maybe too uptight. None of us should become so rigid in the details of how we live that we lose sight of our overall goal of service.

But like Jim and his few pounds, we need to ask ourselves whether our "lawful" activities are really "expedient" in our service to God.

The Prodigal Daughter

"He came to himself"

Luke 15:17

The story of the prodigal son (Luke 15:11-32) is one of Jesus' most beloved parables. You remember that the younger son asked his father to give him his inheritance early. He took the money, went into "a far country," and spent it all on partying and wild living.

When he ran out of money and had nothing for food, he started taking care of pigs for a farmer and even ate some of the pig's food for nourishment. Then in the words of the beautifully classical King James Version of the Bible we read these significant words understood by all who have had this experience, "he came to himself." He had evaluated his miserable situation and decided to do whatever it took to return to his father. To his surprise, his father welcomed him with joy and threw a party in his honor. It was so much more than he could have expected.

It occurred to me that in some ways, my journey down the organizational pathway paralleled his. I had lived in an orderly and harmonious house as a child. When I left home to establish my own home, to my surprise I found myself in an unexpectedly disorganized life, a far country indeed from my former life. For years, without realizing what I was doing or the consequences of my actions, I had broken every rule of organizing in the book. Like the prodigal son, the seriousness of my messy house and life was unpleasant and eventually became desperate.

But thankfully, eventually I "came to myself" as he had done and I evaluated my situation clearly. "Others don't struggle with clutter like I do," I told myself. "Somehow I have got to find a way to return to the kind of life I knew as a child in my organized mother's home."

The way back was uncharted. But slowly I discovered the ideas, rules, and routines that all organized people follow. To some they come naturally. Others, like me have to learn them by rote and practice them until we get them right.

One step at a time I began to return to the wonderful way of life I had known as a child. Like the prodigal son, this new way of life has been so much more than I had expected and I have been celebrating more and more every day since then.

If you have wandered away, even ever so slightly from the order and beauty that can be yours, join me on the path back to a life of harmony and beauty.

Name some ways you have come to yourself in the area of organizing.

Rejoice in any insights you have developed.

Stop and ask yourself, "Is there an area in which I think I cannot live like this anymore"? That is where you still need to "come to yourself".

⑨ *A Beautiful Life*

"Wisdom makes life pleasant and leads us safely along. My child, use common sense and sound judgment! Always keep them in mind. They will help you to live a long and beautiful life."

Proverbs 3:17, 21, 22 (CEV)

Like picking three kinds of flowers from a garden, let's ask ourselves three questions related to this verse

❀   What do we want?
The answer is clear from the text. We want a pleasant life, a long and beautiful life. Furthermore we want to be led safely along in a life without unpleasant surprises or dangers. Or as the stately language of the King James Version states it, when we find them "they shall be life unto thy soul."

❀   Where can we find these things?
The answer to that question is also very clear. "Wisdom," "common sense and sound judgment" will help us live the harmonious life we yearn for. These three are free to anyone who seeks them in that most reliable of all sources of wisdom, the Bible.

❀   How do we tap into this wisdom, common sense and sound judgment?
We are told they will help us if we "use" them and "keep them in mind." More literally, the Hebrew tells us, "Do not let them out of your sight." (Proverbs 3:21 NIV)

In addition to telling us the way to heaven and how we can be right with God through Jesus, God's word instructs us in many ways about how to live a long and beautiful life on this earth.

As always reading is not enough. We need to do more than observe these three flowers. We must plow God's admonitions into our thought lives and let them flow out through our actions.

❀ *Apply to your life* ❀

In relation to your life how do you define a beautiful life?

Study Proverbs, God's gems of wisdom, and find wise ideas to follow.

10 Following Esau

"...Esau, who for one morsel of food sold his birthright..."

Hebrews 12:16

Poor Esau! He made a really bad decision. You remember the story told in Genesis 25. Esau went hunting to kill something for food but came home with an empty bag and hungry stomach. He felt like he was starving.

His wily younger brother, Jacob, offered to trade him some of his hot dinner if Esau would transfer to him the birthright due Esau as the older brother. Esau made the trade, exaggerating his need for food and forgetting about the future. As a result, his whole life changed. Esau has become the poster boy for short sighted decision making, trading an immediate want for a long term benefit.

Isn't that what we do when we keep or buy something we want on the spur of the moment even though it interferes with our long term desire for a simpler and more orderly life?

A magazine, a trinket, a souvenir -- we pile it to the side without thinking because we want it at that moment. One spontaneous decision after another sweeps away any orderly clear surface we may have desired.

Like Esau, we may have traded a temporary "fix" for long term satisfaction of an orderly home.

There are many Jacobs in our lives catching us when we are weak and encouraging us to respond to our present desire even when it destroys what we really want and need.

Keep your long term desire for a beautiful and harmonious home in mind. Overcome urges to buy, accept, keep, rescue, or otherwise harbor things in our lives that in the end harm the way of life we are striving for.

Avoid being like Esau. Tell your Jacob to take a hike. You are hanging on to your birthright of an orderly home no matter how great the temptation to do otherwise.

❦ *Apply to your life* ❧

What can you do to avoid getting distracted and maintain your important, long term priorities in mind?

Replace hunger for stuff with a desire for your real birthright – a beautiful life.

Close your eyes and envision the home you want. Hold onto that vision.

11 *Do It for Love*

"God is not unjust; he will not forget your work and the love you have shown him as you have helped his people and continue to help them."

Hebrews 6:10

Love is not just a feeling, a good intention, a hope for the best. Love is shown in what we do to help others. The King James translation of this verse calls it a "labor of love." The work we do for others shows love to God.

It amazed Delores to see how much other women in the church seemed to be able to do. When someone was sick, they seemed to be able to whip something together and deliver it (with their neatly dressed children in tow.) During vacation Bible school they were right in there decorating and teaching. Though she did her best when she could, she often sat out opportunities she wanted to participate in because she was just too disorganized to be able to do it.

Like Delores, sometimes we can't get our act together enough to actively give the help we want to. In order to help others we need to be prepared. We must have the things we need, the knowledge we need, the time we need. Often that translates into making adjustments to be able to accomplish our goal.

To do that we need to:

Choose - We can't help everybody do everything. Select an area where you are going to concentrate your efforts.

Prioritize - Cut the fat. Drop unproductive behaviors and clutter of life that slow you down. Spotlight the things that will move you successfully forward.

Inaugurate - Set up a plan to accomplish what you have chosen to do.

Prepare - Gather the materials, block out time, learn what needs to be done and how to do it, and engage other helpers if necessary.

Initiate - Actually begin to act. Talk is cheap. God rewards successful action backed by a loving heart, not shallow intentions.

Why do we do these things? We do it to show we love God as we help his people. Behind it all, he is watching and he won't forget what you have done for him through them.

❧ *Apply to your life* ☙

Name something you do not do on a regular basis that you would like to do as a "labor of love" for others.

Inventory your skills and talents. Think of how to use them for others.

12 *Too Important to Stop Now*

"I am doing a great work, so that I cannot come down."

Nehemiah 6:3, 4

Distractions. Unfinished jobs. Neglected items of business. It happens to us all. But letting these hindrances overtake us to any great degree will wreck any successful accomplishments we are pursuing. Only strong concentration and commitment to what is really important will keep us on the right path.

Nehemiah's enemies tried to distract him from his job. They gave him compelling reasons to quit for an important meeting with them but he refused to slow down or leave his work.

His words reveal his state of mind clearly. In a more contemporary version than the one above we read that he says, "So I sent messengers to tell them, 'My work is too important to stop now and go there. I can't afford to slow down the work just to visit with you.' They invited me four times, but each time I refused to go." (Nehemiah 6:3, 4 CEV) Finally they threatened him but he just prayed for strength and kept working.

We have got to admire someone who has focus this strong and sticks with it even under pressure. What was his job? Something very like the work we do on a daily basis in our homes in that it was physical labor that needed to be done. Nehemiah was rebuilding a broken wall to keep the city of Jerusalem safe. Daily, or weekly, we work in our homes to give our families a haven from the outside world.

When it is for an important purpose, physical labor, putting one foot in front of another, one block on another, and in our case in modern living, one task after another, becomes very important. It becomes a great work. Our work becomes too important to stop.

Let Nehemiah become our model. We have many daily jobs, projects, and household goals. Decide what is important to you to do and then stick with it no matter what distractions may come. Say to yourself and to others, "My work is too important to stop now." If it's God's job for you, your "great work" of the moment, finish it before you wander off to tend to something else.

ᘒ *Apply to your life* ᘓ

What are the chronic distractions in your life that keep hindering you from doing what you think is important?

Why is your work in the home a "great work"?

List some ways to say "No" to distractions. Post them by your phone.

13 Freely Give

"Freely ye have received, freely give."

Matthew 10:8

When Jesus commissioned the twelve disciples for service and sent them out on their mission to serve, he added, "Freely ye have received, freely give." He expanded his meaning by telling them not to take any money or additional supplies like coats, shoes, or food.

Echoing instructions in the Old Testament, Jesus said "It is more blessed to give than to receive." (Acts 20:35)

Wow! Talk about not being materialistic! These men heard a message that echoes down to us today:

Having lots of stuff is unimportant.

Giving is natural to followers of Jesus.

Our focus should be our mission in the world.

Giving is better than getting.

Jesus set the example for us by not having much of this world's goods. He did not have much to give materially because he never set out to gather much. Instead, he gave himself in service during his short life and as a culmination sacrificed his life for others.

Look around. Make an enthusiastic commitment to give. What do you have in your closet, your garage, and the rooms of your house that you can give away? Often we give away things we have never used or never even liked in the first place. That is fine. But you can also give away things you like. The point is to unhook yourself from materialistic attitudes that make you want to keep way too much stuff while denying it to others with whom you could share.

Plan to be a giver. Tuck a "Give Away" box permanently in some out of the way place in your house so that you can quickly drop in items to be taken to charity on a regular basis. Then ferry them there, laughing as you go, remembering the words of Paul in 2 Corinthians 9:7, "Every man according as he purposeth in his heart, so let him give; not grudgingly, or of necessity: for God loveth a cheerful giver."

CB *Apply to your life* &O

Do you have a permanent "Give Away" box in your house? If not, where would you put one if you decided to have one?

Keep the donation receipts for tax deductions.

Find out places to drop off donations or get the number to call to have the items picked up.

Plan to give away a similar item every time you buy a new one.

14 *Everything is Beautiful*

"He hath made everything beautiful in its time..."

Ecclesiastes 3:11

God himself is beautiful. The descriptions of his presence in heaven show him upon a throne, glowing in colors, and surrounded by splendor. Sometimes in trying to describe his beauty, we say God is glorious, sometimes majestic, and sometimes we speak of his splendor.

Not only is God beautiful, everything God creates is beautiful. He sets great store by beauty. When he gave instructions for the building of the temple, the plans reflected him in a resplendent way.

Through Isaiah he speaks of a time on earth when people will bring items "to beautify the place of my sanctuary; and I will make the place of my feet glorious." Isaiah 60:11

Yes, beauty is important to God. Everything he touches in a creative way veers toward loveliness. That is why it is so important that as we work to bring order to our homes we continue working until we have brought beauty out of the ashes of what was once clutter.

A pretty environment cannot be built on disorder. It rises from an orderly foundation. So first get rid of clutter by discarding excess and storing what is important. Then move on to creating an environment of loveliness and grace. Look at the homes of your friends. Go to model homes. Check out magazine pictures. Look into your own heart for what you would like to see. But don't stop until you have created a place of harmony for yourself, your family, and your friends. And don't forget to include God in what you are doing because, as you know, God likes beauty.

CZ *Apply to your life* ℘

What is the most beautiful spot in your house at the moment? Thank God for the ones you do have!

Is there a spot you want to beautify now?

Write a goal for what you want, post it.

15 An Ancient To-Do List

And the king said, What honor and dignity hath been done to Mordecai for this? Then said the kings servants that ministered unto him, There is nothing done for him."

Esther 6:3

When I returned from several weeks away from home, I began thumbing through back notes I had made before the trip about projects and other activities I had been working on. I saw several things I had forgotten that I was in the midst of doing.

As I perused the pages, suddenly I was transported in my thinking to a similar scene in the Bible. When King Xerxes, had insomnia (recorded in Esther 6:1-3), he decided to look back over his project journal that's called "the book of the records of the chronicles." Looking back he realized he had not completed one of his projects-- rewarding Mordecai for reporting a plot against his life.

The ancient king and I had something in common. We both kept records of our "To-Do" activities. And we both checked back over our lists to make sure nothing has fallen through the cracks.

The reason this list/journal method has lasted over the millennia is because it is a standard, tried-and-true method that really works. Are you part of this historical and useful method? If not, join us -- the king and I. Keep a To-Do list and check it till the projects in the works get done.

ೞ *Apply to your life* ೦

If you haven't already got one, start a To-Do list to keep projects from falling through the cracks.

If you already have a To-Do list, but it is not working for you, take a look at how you use your list. Does it have outdated projects on it that are holding you back from moving forward?

Is it organized into categories that will help you accomplish the tasks? For example,

Things to do in the home

Telephone calls to make

Things to do away from home

Make your list work for you.

16 Just Get Started

"As soon as the priests who carried the ark reached the Jordan and their feet touched the water's edge, the water from the upstream stopped flowing."

Joshua 3:15b-16a

When the children of Israel crossed the Jordan River into the Promised Land, the priests carried the Ark of the Covenant right to the flowing current that stood in their way. Once their feet touched the water's edge, the water stopped flowing and the ground across dried up.

It happens that way with me a lot, it seems. Often an impossible job begins to melt away once I take the first step to begin it. I may not know exactly how I will accomplish it before I start, but just beginning starts the ball rolling toward success.

Apply this organizing principle. Even if you don't see the details of how all of the project will get done, just get going on it. As you take one step at a time, the next step will become clear and soon you will find yourself on the other side of the Jordan (oops! I mean the project.)

∞ *Apply to your life* ∞

Do you have a project you have been hanging back on doing because you can't see all of the steps to getting it done?

What would be the first step toward that goal? Are you willing to take that step?

Is there someone who has already done a similar project who can give you advice on the next step to take?

17 Oh No! The Loss of All Things

Biblical Christians hold belongings very lightly. At least, we are supposed to if we heed the example of the followers of Jesus and of Jesus himself.

Jesus said he had no home, no place to lay his head (Matthew 8:20) Paul said that for Jesus he had "suffered the loss of all things and do count them but refuse that I may win Christ." (Philippians 3:8)

Jesus told the story of the man who built bigger barns to hold his accumulating crops and called him a fool for focusing on physical things and ignoring the more important spiritual aspect of life.

Time after time we see the concept of holding life's belongings lightly acted out in the early church. The first believers sold property in order to have money to share with the needy. (Acts 4:32-37). In the book of Hebrews, believers are exhorted to count the confiscation of their property a joy during their time of persecution.

Paul reminds us that we brought nothing into the world and, perhaps with a smile, reminds us that we will take nothing out. Be content with having just food and clothes, he tell us in his letter to Timothy. (1 Timothy 6:7, 8)

We are not all called upon to become itinerant proclaimers of the gospel. In their travels Jesus and others stayed in the homes of believers who used their homes to support their ministries. Nonetheless, this does not negate the obvious emphasis on the concept that "things" should be relatively unimportant in the lives of believers.

For those of us who overdo keeping things because we are sentimental, fear not having what we need in the future, or need them for creative projects, or other reasons, this concept challenges something dear to our hearts.

Nonetheless, like an unrelenting fire, the concept of de-emphasizing the goods of this world burns through the New Testament, through the ages, and into our hearts today. Tough as it is, we are called upon to embrace the thought that a person's life does not consist in the abundance of things he (or she) possesses. Then, as always, we are called upon to act on that idea in whatever way that works out in our lives.

God give those of us who struggle with this concept the grace to unclench the hand that holds too tightly that which perishes. Shine the light of eternity into the cluttered cubicles of our hearts and minds.

18 The Simple Things

"that we may live peaceful and quiet lives in all godliness and holiness."

1 Timothy 2:2 (NIV)

Wild living is in vogue in today's world. Music and entertainment of all kinds strive to go from one excess to another. The word "Extreme" is used to sell everything from sporting events to clothes.

Being "on the edge" and "out of control" excites the modern mind. People buy to excess, party to excess, vacation to excess, watch movies that get the adrenaline flowing --- well, you get the idea. Frenetic living rules the day. It's easy to get caught up in the atmosphere that surrounds us.

This causes trouble in Orderland. Common things in life like paying bills, loading the dishwasher, commitments in relationships, remembering birthdays tend to get lost in the confusion of all this excitement.

Like a slap in the face of wild living are Paul's words to Timothy to pray for everyone, especially for those in authority (those appointed to keep order) so that we may go quietly and humbly about our business.

The Christian mindset and goal is to strive for "tame living." Then we can take pleasure in the simpler things of life. The stage will be set to live orderly and profitable lives. Our influence will be good for our children, family, and friends.

Society will benefit from our way of life. We will find satisfaction at how living this way pays off in the long run. But most of all, God will be pleased.

○§ *Apply to your life* §○

Turn off all the noise in your home and sit for 5-10 minutes.

What are several quiet and peaceable things you do that keeps your life organized?

19 *The Place of Prayer*

"Send me good speed this day..."

Genesis 24:12

Eliezer had an assignment from his master, Abraham. Abraham sent him on a journey to find a wife for his son Isaac, sort of a mail-order bride with special delivery. It was an important job because through Isaac would flow the blessing of God on the Jewish nation. The chosen woman would be in ancestral lineage of Jesus who was to come as the Messiah.

But Eliezer didn't know who to choose. So he did what he needed to do. He prayed that God would give him success.

"And he said, O Lord God of my master Abraham, I pray thee, send me good speed this day..." (Genesis 24:12)

If you know the story you know that God did show him the right woman for Isaac and they assumed their roles in God's long term plan for the world.

Eliezer had a goal worth praying about. What he was doing was bigger than just one couple's happiness.

Organizing our houses is like that for us. Though it may seem mundane, it is more than putting up this and cleaning up that. It is creating an atmosphere where we can strengthen our spirits and that of our families. More than that, we are designing a space and a way of life that supports our ministry to others. Let's ask God to give us success.

❧ *Apply to your life* ☙

Is your goal, like Eliezer's, important enough to pray about? You can pray about the work of each day knowing it is an important part of God's plan for your life.

What do you want to pray about today?

Can you write a simple prayer here?

20 *Serve with Strength*

"If anyone serves, he should do it with the strength God provides, so that in all things God may be praised through Jesus Christ."

1 Peter 3:11 NIV

None of the modern viewpoint that the most important person to take care of in the world is *me* slips into Peter's exhortation. Peter observed the behavior of Jesus who lived a life of service to others. Jesus had taken a towel and, doing the job of a servant, had washed their feet. He specifically told them that those who wanted to be leaders must be servants.

Of course, there is a balance. Jesus took time to refresh himself with solitude, prayer, and rest. He had companions to sustain himself in a social context. His friends fed and housed him. But there is no getting around it. One of the favorite things God wants us to do is to serve.

Any project can be hard for those of us to whom organizing does not come easy because everything we do has steps for accomplishment. Many also require collecting equipment to get the jobs done (like finding car keys.) Getting our organizational act together enough to help others may not be easy. But it is required.

Look at what Peter says in this passage: (1 Peter 4:7-10)

♦ Be clear minded and self-controlled

- Love each other deeply
- Offer hospitality without grumbling
- Use whatever gift he has received to serve others
- Faithfully administering God's grace in its various forms

We have a choice of what way we are going to serve and what form of grace we are going to administer. We are all gifted differently and are capable in different areas. But we have no option about serving; that's a given.

❧ *Apply to your life* ❧

Don't try to serve in a way that is unnatural or impossible for you. As best you can, pursue a clear-minded and self-controlled life. Then using your strength seek God's strength to serve others to the glory of God.

Inventory your talents and then use those to serve others.

21 Grow Wise

"He who walks with the wise grows wise."

Proverbs 13:20a

A woman told me of her unique way of learning how to organize. Her family had some friends whose organizing skills she admired. Because they were desperate and had no clue how to rise out of their cluttered way of life, from time to time they would visit her neat friends as house guests for the sole purpose of watching how she accomplished order so successfully.

"Just keep doing what you usually do," she said to her hostess, "and we will watch." And they stood back and observed.

So with an eye to learning wisdom from their hostess, little by little the family learned effective new ways of doing things.

Maybe you and I don't have an accommodating friend we can move in with on occasion but we can still learn from those who are wiser than about organizing. We can read books, go to classes, and visit with organized friends. In my book, The Messies Manual, I tell about my experience of mining the thoughts of my organized friends by asking them their secrets. Maybe you can even think of a knowledgeable friend who will come over to your house and give you advice -- or possibly even work with you as you seek order and beauty in your home.

❦ *Apply to your life* ❧

What is a good source of wisdom for you?

Do you have a wise friend with whom you can walk down the organizing path so you can grow wise as well?

22 A Time to Throw Away

"A time to keep, and a time to throw away."

Ecclesiastes 3:?

Thank God for the seasons of life. The farmer does. He does not have to plow the ground for planting, plant, tend the crops with fertilizer and water, reap and store and then, sell the crops all in one month. In the plan of God, all of these things come in an orderly sequence.

We do well to take a clue from nature and from this passage in Ecclesiastes. Solomon tells us, "To everything there is a season, a time for every purpose under heaven." (Ecclesiastes 3:1)

He expands this idea later by saying that there is "A time to keep, and a time to throw away." (Ecclesiastes 3:?)

How can we tell when is the time to throw away or to give away?

+ When you run out of room for easy storage

+ When it is broken and it is unreasonable to fix it (or you just haven't fixed it for a long time.)

+ When it doesn't fit anybody any more

+ When it is part of a broken set (game with pieces missing, one ear ring)

+ When you don't really like it any more or maybe never did

55

- When you are keeping it "just-in-case."

- When it is a duplicate

When we are young, furnishing our homes and raising our children our lives are very different from when our nest is empty and later when we are retired. Different seasons require very different items to support what we do in that stage of life. It makes sense that we change the items we need to correspond with the seasons of our lives.

ೞ *Apply to your life* ೕ

Do the items in your life match your present season?

Is there any thing you need to throw away or give away?

23 *Abounding*

"Therefore, my beloved brethren, be ye steadfast, unmovable, always abounding in the work of the Lord, forasmuch as ye know that your labor is not in vain in the Lord."

1 Corinthians 15:58

The word "abounding" is a happy active word. It makes us think of jumping (or bounding) from one mountain peak to another, making lots of progress easily.

Let's step personally into this picture. Envision what you want to do in the work of the Lord, how and where you want to abound. Perhaps it involves church work, perhaps nurturing the family, possibly entertaining and fellowshipping as the Bible tells us to do.

If we have this energetic desire to do God's work, we don't want to be hindered, to stumble in our forward progress in doing what is good.

That is why being organized makes such good sense for us; organization strengthens us to abound, to "give ourselves fully to the work of the Lord" (NIV) so that our efforts will not be in vain.

ೞ *Apply to your life* ೞ

What would you do if you were to "abound" in the way you want to?

24 Abundance of Things

"Not in the abundance of the things he possesses."

Luke 12:15

Jesus had a lot to say about possessions. Often he urged us to regard them lightly. In this case he said plainly, "One's life does not consist in the abundance of the things he possesses." (Luke 12:15b) NKJV

Umm, this relates to my way of thinking about possessions. I wonder what would happen if I just tossed (gently, of course) some of those unopened boxes packed long ago. Or told a hauling company, "Just clear out all the stuff in this shed," without looking through it (well, maybe just a light glance.)

"One's life does not consist in the abundance of things he possesses." If I could internalize this thought I could do whatever it takes in whatever way is appropriate in my case to live free of clutter.

Right after saying this, Jesus told the story of a man who worked hard to gather abundance for himself. When he died shortly after attaining his goal, God asked "then whose will be those things which your have provided?"

Dying presents a final dilemma for the person with too many possessions. Not that we mind that final letting go. Death gives relief from the burden we have borne for so long. But we leave our families with our problem.

When regarded from this standpoint we ask ourselves, "What importance is all this stuff in my life today? Not only does it not add to my life, it crushes out the vitality."

In the final part of the story, Jesus contrasts having riches on this earth with being rich toward God. That concept strikes a chord. Could I have so much satisfaction in my soul from my relationship with God that I would begin to see these trinkets, papers, mementos, and projects as the unsatisfying things that they are and be willing to let them go?

As the song says, when I turn my eyes upon Jesus and look full in his wonderful face, the things of earth will grow strangely dim in the light of his glory and grace. Let's make this our theme song.

25 Abundant Life

"I am come that they might have life and that they might have it more abundantly."

John 10:10

The "more abundant" life is something God wants us to have. Knowledge that our sins are forgiven and we stand before a holy God because of Jesus' sacrifice brings more abundant life, the spiritual life. He has assured that those who trust in Jesus as Savior will step into the place he has prepared for us in Heaven and that will definitely be abundant life!

In the meantime, on this earth we have a life to live. What kind of life will it be? Surely, the concept of having abundant life applies to the present life we live here and now as well. Our heart tells us that it is right to seek lives of dignity and fullness. Our spirit tells us that the godly life is not the jumbled and stressed life which is frequently a part of disorganization.

Somewhere hidden in this verse is the approval of God on our organizational efforts, our desire to live our best, most abundant life. When we are doing what we feel God wants us to do, we can count on his assistance.

Don't get me wrong. Sometimes unusual circumstances or other priorities dwarf the issue of organization. Living an orderly life may be impossible in certain disasters or conditions. But for most of us, most of the time getting rid of clutter and learning good organizational skills will help us think clearly and enjoy the life circumstances God has given us.

CB *Apply to your life* BO

Thank God for the abundant life he has provided in both the spiritual realm and in our everyday activities.

Ask for his help in participating in this abundance more and more.

26 Spirit of Wisdom

"I have chosen Bezalel...and I have filled him with the Spirit of God, with skill, ability, and knowledge in all kind of crafts--to make artistic designs for work in gold, silver, and bronze...and to engage in all kinds of craftsmanship. I have appointed Oholiab...to help him."

Exodus 31:2-6

The reason we don't go directly to heaven as soon as we establish a relationship with God through Jesus is that God has a purpose for our being on earth. To accomplish that purpose he has given us all some kind of ability, a wisdom of some special kind. Wisdom does not always have to do with intelligence of the scholastic kind. Bezalel was wise in how to work to produce crafts.

You are wise in ways that many others are not. You have certain skills that God wants you to use for him. Perhaps they relate mostly to doing things with your hands such as knitting and cooking or with hammering and sawing. It could have to do with communication in speaking or writing, perhaps technical ability of some kind. Maybe you are a good organizer. Or a myriad of other skills, all of which are necessary for humans as they work together for the glory of God.

Woodrow Kroll of Moody Bible Institute tells the story of Jimmy Durante, an entertainer during World War II, who committed to speaking to a group of troops for five minutes during a stopover in a tour of the war zone. However, he continued his act for thirty minutes to the delight of his audience of war weary soldiers. He explained why he had extended his act. "See those two injured guys sitting together in the front row, one missing his right arm and one his left? They have been clapping together for me using the one arm they have. I couldn't stop."

So it is with the church of God. Find your ability, find a way you can use it for God, and find someone else you can combine your skill with to fulfill the purpose you have been left on the earth. Don't let anything hinder you from clapping your biggest for the glory of God.

❧ *Apply to your life* ☙

Where does your spirit of wisdom lie in your life?

What can you do for the glory of God?

27 *Teach Us to Number Our Days*

"Teach us to number our days and recognize how few they are; help us to spend them as we should."

Psalm 90:12 TLB

When a single marble fell out of the pocket of my jacket, I remembered where I had gotten it. Walt had given me that marble from his pocket as we chatted after church. Sometimes he brought them to church to give to the children.

"This was last week," he said referring to the marble. "It was a pretty good week."

Then he explained what he meant. He had estimated (I supposed using actuarial tables) how many more weeks he could expect to live and put a marble for each week into a jar. Every Sunday he removed a marble from the jar and watched the pile shrink. It encouraged him to realize the importance of each day. Sort of his version of "It's a Wonderful Life."

Talk about a time management concept! We have an opportunity to do important things that need to be done. But that time is limited. For Christians, our jar of marbles stands for the life God has put within us.

The psalmist tells us, "Teach us to number our days and recognize how few they are; help us to spend them as we should (Psalm 90:12 TLB)

Walt's approach does not appeal to me! It seems kind of grim, actually. But his idea makes a good point:

If we stop to think about it, as we do very seldom, we can look at Walt's visual approach of our dwindling lives in a positive way, a cozy reminder that we have a bunch of wonderful marbles to spend in whatever way we wish.

Therefore, the best thing to do is to ask God to do for us the same two things the psalmist prayed:

- Teach us to number our days
- Help us to spend them as we should

Umm, maybe a jar of marbles would be a good idea, then again --- maybe not.

❈ *Apply to your life* ❈

How can you concentrate on the value of each day so that you can use each to the max?

28 The Serenity Prayer

God grant me the serenity to accept the things I cannot change; courage to change the things I can; and wisdom to know the difference.

(Often used by twelve step programs)

Marilyn's life was full of turmoil because of her disorganized lifestyle. Bills went unpaid because of faulty money habits. She didn't know for sure how much was in her account or exactly where she had put the bills. She worried that she would miss appointments either because she had failed to write them down or had forgotten to check the calendar. The house looked too messy for company and she often misplaced keys, shoes, and other items.

Though she bore up under the strain bravely and struggled to keep her life moving forward, from time to time the burden seemed to overwhelm her and, being a Christian, she asked God to help her and to give her peace in the midst of the turmoil she lived in. In a way she was praying the serenity prayer.

The prayer now called the serenity prayer falls into three boxes.

- ◆ The first box is filled with things that can't be changed. When we open that box we need serenity to face them. That peace is what she sought.

- The second box contains things that we can change. When we open that box, we need courage. Behavior change is a daunting challenge.

- The third box contains discernment, the wisdom to know which of the first two boxes we need to dig into.

After she looked into the third box, Marilyn realized she had been opening the wrong box. Peace of heart is not what she needed. She needed a serious change of behavior. The unrest in her heart about her disorganization was a gift to prod her to live differently.

So Marilyn closed the first box where she asked for serenity and began digging into the second box of courage for the long journey of changing her way of life. Slowly but surely she addressed and changed the areas of turmoil in her life and one day she looked back and noticed, the box of serenity had opened wide.

✃ *Apply to your life* ✄

Ask again for courage to change the things you can.

29 Burned Up! Destroyed?

"The day of the Lord will come like a thief, in which the heavens will pass away with a roar and the elements will be destroyed with intense heat, and the earth and its works will be burned up. Since all these things are to be destroyed in this way, what sort of people ought you to be?"

2 Peter 3:10:11

If I knew that all of my things would be destroyed in a fire, would I still want to gather so much stuff? Well, I have it on good authority in the passage above that all of our stuff is destined for incineration.

Thinking about this passage and all the belongings he and his wife have collected in their years of marriage, Chuck Swindoll says "we travel too heavy and live too encumbered."

Our relationships are often neglected or even harmed by our over commitment to things. Pure relationships and clear vision are weighed down by irrelevancies accumulated in life and time.

North America is the one place in the world with the worst weather. Add to hurricanes, lightning, blizzards, floods, and tornados and other natural disasters like fires or earthquakes compounded by broken dams and levees and we see possibilities for disaster.

People who lose their belongings in catastrophes often say that they will never value things in the same way they did before they were all whisked away unexpectedly. They turn their attention to more important things like their relationships with others or their important place in the world.

If we could see the temporal nature of things, we would have a different attitude toward them. We would get and keep less. Our time use would be different. As Peter asks in the passage above, "What sort of people ought you to be?"

೦ช   *Apply to your life* ಐ

Life is temporary. What are your thoughts regarding the temporary nature of your belongings?

30 *Don't Drift Off the Path*

"Be careful to obey all the law my servant Moses gave you; do not turn from it to the right or to the left, that you may be successful wherever you go."

Joshua 1:7 (NIV)

God's words to Joshua as he entered the Promised Land are meant for all of us. Never fail to obey God's word, this scripture tells us. Don't turn aside in any way. It is so easy to get sidetracked!

When God told Joshua to commit to following him without deviating, he stated an important principle for success in any endeavor -- stay on track.

This principle has broader application as well. Once you commit to something important such as getting your house and life organized, stick with it until you reach your goal. Organizing is a tough job. Don't lose your resolve and move on to something else that is easier and perhaps more interesting. Take a cue from God's words to Joshua. Stay on the path you committed to until you are fully successful.

❧ *Apply to your life* ❧

Is there some wonderful path you can commit to follow today until you are successful?

Perhaps you have strayed from your path, gotten sidetracked from your plan. Regain your resolve and find the way back to your path. (We may have to do this daily!)

31 *Instant In Season and Out of Season*

"Be diligent in season, out of season"

2 Timothy 4:2

Paul exhorts his young friend, Timothy, to be diligent to do the work God had for him to do. That work was to preach the word. We all have a certain amount of opportunity to work for the Lord. It is our responsibility to really throw ourselves into what we feel God wants us to do, whatever it is.

The writer of the hymn, "Onward, Christian Soldiers," Sabine Baring-Gould had two organizational rules to explain his very productive life. He said that:

- When he had begun a task he stuck to it until it was done.

- He never waited for "inspiration", but plunged ahead with determination in his work. He said that he often did his best work when he least felt like doing it.

And what were his accomplishments?

He owned 3,000 acres of land and held an important government position. He wrote a fifteen volume set of "Lives of the Saints" and "Curious Myths of the Middle Ages" and "Legends of the Old Testaments." He also wrote many other learned books, and devotional writings and volumes of sermons. He was a very popular novelist producing about a volume a year. In total, he wrote more than seventy-three titles, all by hand without a secretary. Amazing!

He wrote other hymns as well as "Onward, Christian Soldiers." One of them which you may know is "Now the Day Is Over."

❧ *Apply to your life* ☙

What do you think about the two rules of Sabine Baring-Gould?

To what extent do you follow either one of them in your life?

32 First This, Then That

*"Finish your outdoor work and get your fields ready;
after that build your house (or barn)."*

Proverbs 25:27 NIV

Most of us are not farmers but we all understand the basic principles of farming. It is wonderful how so many of them apply to our modern day activities. This proverb applies to time and project management.

Two principles are spotlighted here:

+ Complete one job before you start another. One characteristic of disorganized people is that they tend to have too many unfinished projects going on at once. Concentrate on finishing one job before you start another project.

+ Put things in proper order. Disorganized people have trouble with what is known as "executive function." That means it is hard for some of the more creative types who do global reasoning to think in terms of linear planning. First plant the crops. After you have that step done, move on to building the barn.

Two lessons are here for us:

+ Plan very carefully. Write down the steps to your goal in a logical order. Get advice if you need some guidance.

+ Rather than have many balls in the air, finish up one project before taking on more.

❦ *Apply to your life* ❧

Finish Up: Look around the house. Is there a project you can finish up right away?

Plan: Do you have a project you would like to begin? Write down the main steps.

33 Refer to Your To-Do List Regularly

"That night the king could not sleep; so he ordered the book of the chronicles, the record of his reign, to be brought in and read to him."

Esther 6:1-3

The to-do list is an ancient memory device. In the passage above it is used by the king to make sure he has done everything he intended to do. Let's take a hint from him.

Your TO-DO list is your memory for changeable daily items basically in four areas, buying, calling, doing, and writing. Perhaps your four basic areas will be different from these.

Fold a piece of writing paper into four squares and label each square with one of the activities like these:

- ◆ BUY (Things you generally do in the car) - Paper clips, bridal present, etc. Take the clothes to the charity store.

- ◆ CALL (Things you do with the phone) - The children's camp, the phone company, make doctor appointment.

- ◆ DO (Special activities at the house, not the usual routine items) - Sew on the red button, get out Easter decorations, change air conditioner filter.

- WRITE (Done at he computer or with a pen and paper) - Return email letters, inquire about class reunion, write thank you note.

You don't want to carry these little details around in your head. Free your mind and write them down.

✂ *Apply to your life* ✂

Note the sample. Using it or one of your own designs, begin writing down activities you want to accomplish.

34 *The Shadow of a Cloud*

"As heat is reduced by the shadow of a cloud, so the song of the ruthless is stilled."

Isaiah 25:5 (NIV)

There are two ways of making change; direct confrontation or more subtly. The subtle method is mentioned in this verse. This poetry from the book of Isaiah uses the picture of a cloud between the sun and earth reducing the heat (of wickedness, in this case) without fail.

Why? Because the flow of heat energy has been interrupted.

Like many Bible verses, we can apply the specific application of this verse to another area, in our case the area of our living a disorganized life. To cool the "heat" of disorganization, what *clouds* do we seek?

The cloud of awareness - Wake up to the condition of the house. Become visually sensitive to and aware of how the present condition works for you.

The cloud of caring - Don't be willing to continue with disorder. It is easy to get used to clutter, to be willing to live with lower standards.

The cloud of knowledge - Each situation requires a special knowledge of what the problems are, of possible solutions, and specific information about methods of organizing, maintaining and storing.

The cloud of routine - Note which few activities give the most reward for your effort. Schedule those few activities to be done daily and a few more to be done weekly. Write these down and post them in an obvious place.

The cloud of consistency - Once you find a routine that works, hold on to it like a dog guards a bone.

These five little clouds, none dramatic in themselves, will cast a cooling shadow from the heat of disorganization into the house that will slowly dissipate disorder because the origin of clutter and disorder will have been removed.

◌ Apply to your life ◌

Of the five little clouds mentioned above, which one(s) do you feel would be most effective in your life?

35 Some Among You Are Idle

"We hear that some among you are idle. They are not busy."

2 Thessalonians 3:11 NIV

Paul has just written a paragraph exerting the Thessalonians to be busy or, to put it another way, not idle. He states, "We were not idle when we were with you." He says he worked "night and day, laboring and toiling." He says he did it in order to be a model in the area of working hard. (2 Thessalonians 3:6-10)

That is when he begins to speak specifically to them telling them that they should work enthusiastically and with vigor. He says it is their clear responsibility.

When I start slacking, I can think of what Paul did. He must have been a very healthy man indeed. But I also have to remember that we each have different energy levels. Physical variations, age, health, and many other factors affect how much we can do, how long we can work, and with what dynamism.

(Sigh) I don't think Paul understands all of the reasons I can't work as hard as he suggests, "Night and day? Laboring and toiling?"

But I will tell you this, the next time I think of taking it easy when there is work I ought to be doing, I will ask myself as the Bible tells us to, "What would Paul do? (WWPD)

✄ *Apply to your life* ✃

What factors make you work most energetically?

Why do you tend to slack off when you should be working?

36 Everything Permissible

"Everything is Permissible"

1 Corinthians 10:23

Christians have a great deal of freedom in Christ. Twice in the same verse, Paul repeats these words, "Everything is permissible."

His example is that they are allowed to eat anything sold in the marketplace. This flew in the face of Jewish dietary laws that limited what God's people could eat under the old covenant.

Paul goes further and challenges devout Christians who taught that it was wrong to eat meat of animals that had been used in pagan worship. "No," he said. "Go ahead and eat whatever meat you want. Gods and goddesses don't exist and God created meat to be eaten. So go ahead and be grateful."

That much is clear. But the story continues with more examples. If somebody, pagan or not, sees you eating the meat or invites you to dinner and tells you this is meat offered to idols, don't eat it. For them, it means that you think idolatry is okay. Why mess up somebody's life, confuse them, just so you can eat a certain piece of meat?

The final thought is this: You've got more than yourself to think about. Use your good judgment. Men and women are living without God and without hope in the world. Everything else fades into insignificance in the light of their need to hear the good news of Christ.

What does this have to do with organizing? Simply this:

"Everything is permissible" -- but not everything is beneficial.

"Everything is permissible" -- but not everything is constructive.

"Nobody should seek his own good, but the good of others."

1 Corinthians 10:23, 24

You are free to live in clutter. As far as I know, God has not set limits on how much junk you collect or where you keep it. You can lose keys and important papers with impunity, I suppose. It complicates your life but it is not a moral issue.

But a further question is "How is it affecting others?" Is your mess keeping you from living your best for others in the world? Is it hurting your husband, wife, children, or friends? Does it limit your own ability to function at your fullest? Don't indulge yourself in irresponsible living just because it is easier or more natural, or even more enjoyable.

෩ *Apply to your life* ෪

Think about it. You are responsible to seek the good of others. Do what you need to do about disorganization in your life in order to reach that goal.

37 Finish the Work

"Now finish the work..."

2 Corinthians 8:11

How many times has this happened to you? You get a wonderful idea for a great project or activity. Perhaps it is for you personally, for your employment, or for your family. It could be something for the church. It could even be something around the house.

Let us say you decided to purchase a needed bookcase. You bought the unassembled kit at the office supply store. Then something happened. Perhaps a few screws were missing from the kit. Perhaps someone you were counting on to help became unavailable. Other things came up and you were distracted. The half done project languished. Now you have several boards, somewhat joined, along with other parts strewn around. We can listen to the words of Paul to the Corinthians, "Finish the work."

In the passage above Paul tells us that the year previous to his writing; the Corinthians had started vigorously to collect money for a group of needy Christians in another city. Paul scheduled to send Titus and two other brothers to pick up the money (they didn't have mail service or bank transfers in those days.) Then he and some others were going to take the relief effort money to the needy Christians.

But somehow over that year the Corinthians had lost their focus and Paul was afraid they would not be ready with the offering. He didn't want them to do a hurried last minute job of finishing the collection. Paul even indicated that the men would be coming early to help them "finish the arrangement." (2 Corinthians 9: 5)

Procrastination and distraction can happen to the best of us. That's why the Bible has a lot to say about finishing jobs. In speaking of discipleship, Jesus says not to start a building project until you are sure you have what it takes to build it. He continued by saying a king who goes to war needs to be sure before he starts that he is well prepared. (Luke 14:28-32)

Speaking of the end of his life, Paul told the Ephesians church leaders that his desire was to "finish the race and complete the task the Lord Jesus has given to me --- the task of testifying to the gospel of the Lord's grace." (Acts 20:24)

CS *Apply to your life* &

Are you a finisher?

Do you maintain consistent dedication to a task until it is finished in a reasonable time?

Whether it is something around the house, a church program or project, or a life commitment, it is good to develop that character trait and remember Paul's admonition, "Now finish the work."

Is there some job that needs to be finished up in your life right now?

38 *Organized Bible Study*

"Study to show thyself approved unto God, a workman who needeth not to be ashamed, rightly dividing the word of truth."

2 Timothy 2:15

Country music fans, and many who are not, may be interested in knowing how country music legend Johnny Cash explained his Bible study time.

He became very interested in the Bible in the second half of his life. Johnny said he had two versions of the Bible, The King James and the New International version. He liked to read and compare passages and study them in commentaries. He used a concordance and the Thompson Chain Reference system that traces and explores any subject through the whole Bible. When he was on the road, he used the Franklin Electronic Bible for which he was a spokesperson.

He also read books left to him by his father-in-law. All are old, many are classics. Some of his favorites were:

- Two different volumes of the life of Christ
- One on the life and times of Paul
- A thirty book set of commentaries on the whole Bible by Lange
- Books of church history and geography of Palestine

He and his wife, June, enrolled in and graduated from a three year Bible study correspondence course.

But perhaps his biggest plus was that he kept a Bible close at hand by his chair, on the plane, or wherever so he could read it between other activities. Johnny Cash's organized approach took Bible study seriously.

❁ *Apply to your life* ❁

You may have a different approach and more up-to-date books. But however you do it, you need to be prepared with books, time, a system, and dedication to read and study the Bible.

39 Forget Not
to Show Hospitality

"Be not forgetful to entertain strangers; for thereby some have entertained angels unawares."

Hebrews 13:2

This is not just a thought or an inspiration. It is a command. For some of us it is one of the most difficult commandments to keep.

"Thereby some have entertained angels unawares," says the Scripture, probably referring most directly to the hospitality Sarah and Abraham showed to the angels who came to deliver the message that they would have a baby of their own. They entertained in an appropriate manner for the nomads they were.

For some of us the experience would be different, I am afraid. We hear a knock at the door in our modern home.

"Hello, Mr. Angel!" we gasp as we stall on the front porch, startled by the shining and the large wings. ("Kids pick up the living room! Dump all of that stuff in the bedroom!" we whisper urgently over our shoulder toward the living room.)

"How can I help you? Does the Lord need something special from me today?" ("Hurry up kids, hurry!")

"Well, I'm not quite ready to do anything extra today. I have so many things to get caught up with. I really wish I could." ("Is it all clear yet, kids? Not yet? Just shovel it all in the back. We'll clean it up later.")

"You have to go..., so soon? Can't you stay a minute longer? Well, can you come back when I'm not so busy? Let me know a little in advance if you can. But I want you to know, I want to serve the Lord in every way I can. Please come back. I'm just not quite ready today." ("Never mind, kids," you sob closing the door. "It's too late this time.")

But it is a life changing experience. Angels will return. They always do. From now on you will be ready to show hospitality to them whether or not they come with wings. Unsaved friends, unexpected visitors from church, family, those who are in need or have come to meet your need will be welcomed.

Your house is not just a changing, sleeping, or eating station. It is a place of hospitality --- hospitality for God.

❈ *Apply to your life* ❈

What can you do to be a more hospitable person?

I'm Gonna Let It Shine

"Let your light to shine before men, that they may see your good works, and glorify your Father, who is in heaven."

Matthew 5:16

The metaphor makes the truth very clear. Christians are a shining light. Our candle has been lit by the spirit of God. We are given the directive that we are to shine with good works so the rest of the world can see and glorify God because of what we do.

But we are in danger of having our light obscured by an unnamed bushel. Perhaps for everyone the bushel is something different. Disorganization was my bushel. Often I couldn't get my act together organizationally in order to do the good works God wanted me to do.

Entertain…in my house? Ha!

Take a covered dish to the needy? That was too much to ask of me. I could hardly get dinner on the table for my family.

Teach a Sunday school class? I found it hard just to get there with my Bible in hand.

Volunteer to sing at a nursing home? No time.

And yet friends of mine were doing all of these things successfully. Their lights were ablaze. Mine sputtered, greatly in need of having its smutty wick trimmed down to a fresh start.

The traditional hymn about our outreach for the Lord called "Let the Lower Lights Be Burning" exhorts the singer to "trim your feeble lamps, my brother, some poor sailor tempest tossed, trying now to reach the harbor, in the darkness may be lost."

We all know the story of the ten virgins who were waiting for the bridegroom to come. (Matthew 25:1-14) All trimmed the wicks of their lamps so their light would be fresh and clear. But, yipes! The five foolish virgins noticed they were in trouble because they were low on oil. I identified with those five virgins who ran out of oil. Because of poor planning they could not join the party when the bridegroom came. They just were not prepared to shine.

Remove the bushel, trim away smutty excess, and make sure you have what you need to burn brightly. You are here for a purpose. If your house were organized and beautiful and if you had an orderly time schedule with time for service, what would you want to do for God? Today is the day to begin to remove whatever keeps you from living out God's purpose in your life.

❧ *Apply to your life* ☙

Evaluate how your candle shines. Does it glow or sputter?

What excesses due you need to trim from your life?

Where are you running low on oil?

41 Do Good to All Men

"And let us not lose heart in doing good, for in due time we shall reap if we do not grow weary. So then, while we have opportunity, let us do good to all men, and especially to those who are of the household of faith."

Galatians 6:9-10 9 (NASV)

Paul is finishing up his letter to the Galatians with a few important instructions. His clear word of instruction, given twice, is "Do good."

Knowing human nature, even if it is redeemed human nature, he addresses the problem of motivation and persistence. He says:

* Don't lose heart
* Don't grow weary

He then tells us when to do it, "while we have opportunity".

The need for organization fairly screams from these phrases. How can we do our best to do good if we aren't organized? "Opportunity" to do good to everybody but especially fellow believers, comes to those who are prepared to take advantage of it.

Michelangelo, the famous Renaissance sculptor, envisioned figures inside the unfinished marble he was working with. He chipped away all of the useless marble until the figures emerged. The Prisoners, housed at the Uffizi Gallery in Florence, Italy, show a series of unfinished pieces he designed to illustrate this concept. Rising from the solid marble, are the unfinished muscular forms of giants who seem to be struggling to be released from their marble prisons.

Like Michelangelo's prisoners, some of us are struggling to be freed from our old disorganized way of life so we can fully participate in the life God had designed for us.

Don't lose heart because you are disorganized and just can't get your act together in order to do the work of God. Little by little, as you are loosed from that bondage you will be able to take advantage of opportunities that come your way.

❦ *Apply to your life* ❦

Today, be mindful of an opportunity to do good for someone.

42 Rod of Moses, Rod of God

"And the LORD said unto him, What is that in thine hand? And he said, A rod."

Exodus 4:2

The familiar is about to become spectacular. To Moses, his rod was nothing extraordinary, just an everyday shepherd's crook. But God wanted to use it to accomplish a miracle. "Thou shalt take this rod in thine hand, wherewith thou shalt do signs." You remember how God turned the rod into a snake as part of persuading Pharaoh to free the Israelites.

What had appeared to be a common shepherd's tool became so much more. Because God had chosen it for his purposes, the rod of Moses became "the rod of God." (Exodus 4:20) The lesson for us is that God can use the ordinary in our lives for significant purposes.

As in Moses' experience, special purposes lurk in other unlikely areas of life. Water becomes wine. A husband and wife rubbing elbows in the daily pursuit of life symbolizes the union of Christ and the church. In God's purposes, a mundane thing like the atmosphere of your house holds potential to do great things for God. The brick and wood creating a house can rise to become a place where children are nurtured, family and friends are comforted, souls are born into the kingdom, and laughter and joy reflect a heavenly home above.

The demarcation between the heavenly and earthly is very thin. We waffle in and out between the two. If we have eyes to see that this is true, we understand that the functions of our daily lives, no matter how commonplace, can be of great significance. God can use the "ordinary" of your home and it can become the rod of God to do wonderful things.

🙰 *Apply to your life* 🙰

Let me ask you directly, "What is that in thine hand?"

What ordinary things can you dedicate for God's use?

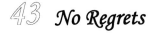

43 No Regrets

"To him who knoweth to do good and doeth it not, to him it is sin."

James 4:17

At lunch my friend and I were discussing goals we had for developing our writing. "I want to get this done," she said. "I don't want to end up a ninety-three year old woman with regrets that I never did it."

"I'm not sure anybody can get to ninety-three and look back without any regrets," I said.

Her reply was very insightful. "That's true but I want my regrets to be for things I did not know to do, not for things I knew to do but didn't."

How close her statement was to James 4:17, "To him who knoweth to do good and doeth it not, to him it is sin."

On a day to day basis, whether it be in the area of how we use our time, how we pay our bills, how we clean our house, how we manage our families, or whatever it is, I do not want my regrets to be that I knew what to do and even how to do it -- but didn't.

What is my hold up for living productively?

- Careless scheduling?

- Poor management skills, especially delegating and supervision?

- Lack of knowledge about "how-to's" of the jobs?

- Lack of dedication and enthusiasm?

- Some other hindrance specific to my circumstances?

Each person needs to choose an approach for accomplishing what he or she knows to do. Maybe I need more education through books or a class on organizing my life. Maybe I need a mentor for guidance and motivation either in person or on line. Maybe I just need to break old, unproductive habits, the hardest change of all.

One thing is clear, like my friend I don't want to look back with regret because I knew full well what I should have done -- but didn't.

❧ *Apply to your life* ☙

When you are ninety-three, what do you want to look back on with satisfaction about a decision you made organizationally?

Good and Faithful Servant

"Well done, good and faithful servant."

Matthew 25: 14-27

Jesus tells a story frequently called the parable of the talents to illustrate an important truth about the kingdom of heaven. Although this well-known story's application is to a broader spiritual truth, it seems to have a practical implication for us in the area of how we organize our houses. Maybe even a direct application.

Most know the story of the man who left his goods to be managed by his three servants. The first two did well. The last, who was none too talented to begin with, did not do well at all. He was supposed to invest the money, to use what he had been given, to improve on it. But he did not.

When I read this story, I thought of the house that the Lord has given me. He left it with me with the expectation that I would improve it. Will I live up to his expectation?

The servant in the story gave as his excuse that he didn't want to take a chance on failing so he just didn't do anything that might not have been successful.

His boss came down really hard on him. He did not buy his excuses. I suspect that man, looking back on it, wished he had been more aggressive in trying even though he was ill suited to do the job and was afraid even to try.

I had little natural talent in organizing my house. I lived with fear of doing it wrong, making the wrong decisions, and numerous other nameless fears that met me at every decision point. If I had thought that in addition to disappointing myself and my family when my house was way out of control I was disappointing God, the idea may have crushed whatever resolve I brought to the problem.

How can we approach the problem of not disappointing God in an area which seems beyond our control? This story holds an answer. The talented servants were initially given a great deal more to manage that the man who was ill prepared to do the job. He was only asked to manage a small amount of money. We can take our clue from that.

Maybe we can limit our area of responsibility. If I can't manage the whole house, I can be a responsible servant in one small area of my house.

Maybe I will dedicate the kitchen sink to him, keep it clean and shining.

Or maybe the dining room table can be kept clear and made beautiful.

Or one little corner of the room cleared. Or the living room area rug kept free of debris. I will try to improve on one small part of the house for his pleasure.

As you do so, be aware that in all things of a practical nature that relate to God, we run the risk of tying our spiritual lives unwisely to earthly things. We tend to go from one extreme to the other, don't we?

If the sink gets dirty, does that mean we have failed God? I doubt it.

If we put a pile of unopened mail on the dining room table, have we disappointed him? Probably not.

You can become a rigid Pharisee that way or end up feeling like a spiritual failure if you go down that road. Worse, you will put your family in the position of trying to live in a shrine. Now there's a scary thought!

Don't do that to yourself or your relationship to him. But do narrow down your area of control to a reasonable size you think you can improve to please him. And go for it!

Perhaps then we will feel a gentle pat on the back, feel a smile, and hear a soft, "Hey, well done, good and faithful servant! I like what you've done there!"

Maybe even a high five and happy dance might be in order.

ᦓ *Apply to your life* ᦑ

In there some small practical way you can begin to act in a more organizationally successful way?

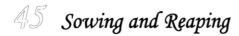 **Sowing and Reaping**

"Whatsoever a man soweth, that shall he also reap."

Galatians 6:7b

Not many of us farm but we all clearly understand the principle of sowing and reaping. What the farmer has stored in his barns at the end of the growing season depends on what he did during the planting season.

In Galatians, Paul applies this farming principle primarily to spiritual life when he speaks of sowing to the flesh and sowing to the spirit in verse 8. However, we can easily see it applies to all of life. What we end up with as a rule depends on the choices we made earlier.

Look around your house. What you see at the end of the day is the result of your earlier actions. The condition of your house at the end of the year depends on what you have been doing to and for your house all year long.

Basically it depends on three things you need to do.

1. Dejunk your house. (Clear that ground!)
The farmer or gardener properly prepares the ground by removing debris. He or she does not try to work around dead stumps or fallen limbs.

Most homeowners keep too much. Dejunk your house by making hard decisions and paring down. Some of the things you have are good. They are just not good for you or for your situation. Throw or give away the excess.

2. Stash your belongings wisely. (Plant those rows!)

Once the field is cleared, he or she puts in the seed in groups, a row of carrots, one of beans, another of tomatoes, etc. They label each row so they can recall what is in each row.

Like the farmer, after you first clear your house of excess and junk, you need to group the belongings you keep into groups and put them in the size container you need. Label the container with signs using large letters. If the grouping is too large for a container (like sports equipment or yard tools), group them together in an appropriate spot and place a label wherever it fits most easily like on a wall or shelf.

If items in the group are used often, put them where they can be easily accessed. If not often used, they can be stored in a place that is harder to reach. If something is not used from year to year but you still want to keep it, stash it in deep storage like the attic or basement.

3. Make a plan to maintain it. (Tend that field, girl!)

Plan, plan, plan. You need some kind of maintenance schedule, preferably a little every day so it doesn't lump up all at once. Then you, and hopefully your field hands, will do what needs to be done to keep things neat and clean.

In addition, you (and they) need to develop habits of putting things back in their place immediately (like books, tools, craft supplies) Move organization forward regularly (like making the bed, cleaning the kitchen after meals, emptying the dishwasher, etc.)

ଔ *Apply to your life* ଊ

The principle is there. Whatever you do right to your house consistently now will inevitably show up in how well it runs and how good it looks later. Act properly. The house will follow.

46 *Thou shalt covet?*

Umm, Yes and No

I thought to covet meant to want something that someone else had as in "Thou shalt not covet thy neighbor's goods." That's definitely one true application. It seems kind of tacky to be envying what other people have and wanting it for myself. So I have tried to avoid that attitude.

To my surprise I learned that it also means just wanting something badly whether anybody else has it or not.

This new discovery gives one pause. Could it be that my "over collecting" might be a result of the ugly characteristic of coveting that I had been trying to avoid. While I was watching the front door trying not to covet other people's things, coveting things in general seems to have sneaked in the back door.

There is no doubt about it. In my case and in the case of most people who struggle with clutter, a very big part of the problem is that we want and have way too many possessions. Way, way too many possessions!

The things we keep seem important to us. We keep things because we think we might need them in the future. Being very smart and imaginative folks we can envision many possibilities of how that might happen such as:

♦

- We keep materials for projects we will get around to doing some day.

- The IRS might descend upon us with questions.

- A child (maybe a neighborhood kid who comes to your door for help) may need it for a costume.

- Or being sentimental and sensible folks who value family history and history in general, we keep for the past like:

- "They don't make skillets like this any more."

- "I loved this as a child."

- "This reminds me of my mother."

When these notions clutch my heart and mind so that I can't let belongings go even though I know I should, they have become items I covet.

On the other hand, the Bible encourages me to covet some good things as in "Covet earnestly the best gifts." (1 Corinthians 12:31) While we are letting go of harmful desires we need to substitute seeking things God wants for us. I think I will decide to covet harmony and order in my home because, to tell you the truth, I do want them very, very much.

❧ *Apply to your life* ☙

Let go of the old desires, grab hold of the new, and life will change.

47 Wherein is Excess

"Be not drunk with wine wherein is excess."

Ephesians 5:18

Paul tells his readers not to get drunk on wine. His reason is fascinating. He says it is excessive. Apparently, he assumes that everybody knows that living to excess should be avoided. It is wasteful and out of control.

The Bible often assumes that those who are committed to living God's way will not live in an excessive way. They will live lives of self-discipline and temperance. In Philippians 4:5, he exhorts "Let your moderation (gentleness, forbearance) be known unto all men."

Repeatedly in the Bible disciplined and wise living is praised for two reasons:

- We have a goal of reaching the world with the gospel and cannot waste time, energy, and resources on unimportant things.

- We walk in faith that God will direct and supply our needs. Satisfaction comes from Him.

Moderation impacts on what we buy, what we keep, how we spend our time and energy, and live in general. Living moderately does not mean we gear down our lives. Rather it means we energetically focus on really important things while devaluing unimportant things.

But we are not fuddy-duddies, sitting home rocking and knitting (though there is a place for that at times.). The Christian life is full, some would even say extravagant. Christians are encouraged to overdo in fellowship, giving, service, joy, singing, and love. Paul summarized it this way, "Be filled with the Spirit." Let that approach control your life and see how a new approach impacts your house and life.

❧ *Apply to your life* ❧

Name a couple of ways you have built moderation into your life successfully.

 *Invigorated Work*

"May our Lord Jesus Christ himself and God our Father... strengthen you in every good deed."

2 Thessalonians 2:16-17 (NIV)

It takes a lot of strength to do all we have to do each day. Energy is not something we should squander on unimportant or unproductive things. Granted, some of the things we use our energy on don't look very consequential when actually they are.

How meaningful are household chores? How important are trips to the store and many other chores? By themselves, they mean little. However, the consequences of not doing them give them significance. As a group, our daily maintenance tasks add up to be very important indeed. If we don't keep up with maintenance, all of life bogs down.

Are these chores the good deeds that the apostle Paul is saying God will give us strength to do? Paul probably did not have taking out the trash or emptying the dishwasher in mind when he penned this line. Though Paul himself was no slacker in daily work as he indicated a few paragraphs later in this book, my guess is he had something more in mind like spreading the gospel, caring for the needy, or studying and teaching the truth of God.

Practicality is this. If we wear ourselves out with daily living activities, we won't have strength to do the more important "good" deeds. So it all works together.

How God does this I don't know for sure. Does he send us strong encouragement that in itself strengthens us? Does he send physical vigor to our tired bodies? Does he send wisdom in how to use our time so we won't dissipate our energy on frivolities? The details are not clear about this.

One thing is clear, however, both "our Lord Jesus Christ himself and God our Father" care enough to "encourage your heart and strengthen you in every good deed and word."

◌ *Apply to your life* ◌

Pray that God will invigorate what you do.

49 *Ask, and It Shall Be Given You*

"Ask, and it shall be given you; seek, and ye shall find; knock, and it shall be opened unto you."

Matthew 7:7

We are encouraged to go to God for help. Using three different verbs we are told to ask, seek, and knock.

So we go to God with our need for help. Let's make our requests specific. It is good to ask for general blessing but when it comes to organizing how about asking for things like:

- the enthusiasm we need to get off to a good start in the morning
- how to keep up with the laundry (explain the hang-up spots)
- wisdom to solve special problems (name the problem)
- guidance in making a schedule
- motivation to do jobs we hate (name the job)

Often we need to take our search for help to others as well as God. We may be surprised at how much help we will get when we ask others to work with us or to give us information to solve problems we are facing. Doors will open as we stop standing helplessly in front of them and actually knock.

Jesus' words encourage us to move out in seeking solutions to our problems.

CB *Apply to your life* BO

Ask God's help today for one specific problem.

Seek help with one specific solution from someone today.

Don't move from where you are until you know what those two items will be.

50 Celebrate Well

"Then all the people went away to eat and drink, to send portions of food and to celebrate with great joy..."

Nehemiah 8:12

Entertaining our friends and family well at a celebration is perhaps the greatest payoff of all our organizational efforts. But it can be one of the hardest because nothing stretches our organizational skills like planning a celebration.

There are many celebrations in the Bible. God commanded Israel to celebrate many important occasions. Jesus told stories of feasts and celebrations as illustrations of the kingdom of God. And, of course, the wedding feast in which the host had planned poorly and run out of wine was where Jesus performed his first miracle.

It seems clear. God likes and wants us to celebrate. Get your house in order. Decorate it for visitors. Make up your to-do list and plan the special foods. Be sure there are enough dishes and silverware. Rent the chairs and tables or borrow them from the church. Send out the invitation to come. Get extra help. Oh, it is a big job all right! But well worth the effort!

Celebrations are important for us as human beings. God knows that and encourages it. Let us do it right and celebrate well!

‍‍ෛ *Apply to your life* ‍‍෩

Do you have an important birthday, anniversary, holiday, or some other important occasion coming up?

Don't let it pass without including friends and family into your home. And don't forget to invite the Lord. He seems to like parties.

51 *Do It With Him*

"Commit your way to the Lord."

Psalm 37:5 NIV

There is a relationship between God and what we do every day, known in this verse as "your way." God cares about how we spend our energy and time. According to Psalm 23, God "leads" and "guides" us in paths during our day.

How would this look in relation to how we keep our house? An imaginary scenario might look something like this:

"Lord, here I am this morning. I want to do your will. Would you like me to sit here and watch television or would you like me to work on getting the house in shape for those thirty minutes instead? Or maybe work while I keep an eye on TV?"

Or "Lord, there is so much to do in the house and I am so busy with other things. Would you like me to fold these clothes, unload the dishwasher, take time to direct the children in tidying, or would you like for me to ignore these things and do something else?"

Or "Heavenly Father, you tell us you want us to show hospitality. With my job and other problems, I don't think I can manage that at this time. Lead me, Father, into your will which maybe down the line will involve having folks in as guests."

Certainly, God's will does not revolve entirely around our doing housework. But part of it does.

Living in chaos and clutter is probably not his best will for us. In addition, it is clear that some things that are definitely God's will for us do require having an organized and harmonious home.

So we go to him for his guidance and help even in the practical matters of life. We do the first things first and, then the second, third, and others follow. Soon our way has led to the kind of harmonious life we want for ourselves and, we suspect, God will lead us to if we commit our way to him.

❧ *Apply to your life* ☙

Use this opportunity and many to come to invite God to be involved in your desires for your house and life.

52 Bread, Wine and Water

When the Lord decided to leave us with ways to make important statements about what we believe, he clothed them in the form of very ordinary things.

His blood was represented by wine, his body by bread, and our identification with his resurrection by using water for baptism. These especially, but other items as well such as seed, coins, sheep, and the like, forever dispel any ideas we may have had that the world of matter and of spirit are totally separate.

Both are intermingled in the ordinances of the church and in the lives we lead in our homes. Our spirits are affected by the kind of homes we have. In hundreds of different ways, a well ordered home speaks to our own souls and to the souls of those who share it with us. It speaks to others about what we believe.

A well-set table and flavorful food says our basic needs are important. Having items well placed and easily accessible so we can find them easily reflects the value of our time. Well-ordered bedrooms and inviting beds indicate we are serious about self care and the care of those we love. In many other ways, what we do in our houses with the daily items of living speaks volumes about what we believe.

೫ *Apply to your life* ೫

Look around your home. The things you see are more than what they seem. They are elements which can become a part of your spiritual life. Dedicate them to him and use them well for his glory.

53 *Covetousness*

(Which is Idolatry)

Paul tells us in his letter to the Colossians that we are to abandon certain characteristics because they are sin. There are several lists of sins in the Bible. In this particular list which consists primarily of sexual sins, Paul ends the list with the sin of covetousness.

"Put to death, therefore, whatever belongs to your earthly nature: sexual immorality, impurity, lust, evil desire, and greed (translated covetousness in the King James Version), which is idolatry." Colossians 3:5 (NIV) Eugene Peterson renders this word loosely in The Message as "grabbing whatever attracts your fancy."

According to Webster's dictionary, "idolatry" means "excessive attachment for some person or thing." Of course, this may be an idol or an image. But it doesn't have to be. It could be our personal belongings.

Let's not push this too far and become aesthetic, denying ourselves things that are a part of God's blessing to us. But it is a strong warning that excessive love of things is wrong.

What does this have to do with organizing our houses? In today's world, having too much is one of the chief difficulties we bump into when organizing. It takes time, effort, and often frustration to deal with our excess. But for many of us, having an overabundance is part of our "earthly nature."

Is it possible to change an integral part of who we are? Paul thinks so. He tells us to "Put to death, therefore, whatever belongs to your earthly nature."

"Oh, no! Go away!" we cry whenever death comes near. Loss hurts, not primarily loss of our things as we pry them out of our lives, but loss of a personal characteristic that is part of who we are.

"I've got to be me" states one song. "I did it my way" belts out another. But quietly between the pages of a black and sometimes dusty book, God tells us there is a better way --- we die to self and live to him.

❧ *Apply to your life* ☙

Do you have any attitudes about your belongings that need to die?

Do you need to obtain less? Get rid of things?

All because God's world, not this one, is the world you want to concentrate on.

54 Why We Were Created

"For we are God's workmanship, created in Christ Jesus to do good works, which God prepared in advance for us to do."

Ephesians 2:10

God has been working on us, changing us through our relationship with Jesus. And what is the reason God has done this? One of the reasons is so that we can do good works.

Apparently he has things he want us to do. We are not on this earth just to enjoy ourselves and, after we become Christians, to enjoy the salvation God has so graciously bestowed on us. No, he wants us to roll up our sleeves and get out in his field and work.

Talk about rolling up sleeves and going into fields is very colorful. Using farming analogy (as Jesus often did) gets the idea across very clearly. However in our modern world working for God shows up in very different ways.

In today's world instead of rolling up our sleeves and going into God's figurative field, we gas the car, email others, study to teach, prepare a meal for someone in need, pray for others, eat lunch with an unsaved friend and many other very non-agrarian activities. All the while we are striving to keep our house in order, our family and ourselves properly fed, our children's needs cared for, our relationships strong --- all of this possibly in addition to holding down a job.

Believers wear two hats, our everyday work hat and God's work hat, representing those good works which God has prepared ahead of time for us to do. Since we wear these two hats, believers must give all the more attention to how we order our lives. God does not want us to be frenetically stuffing more into an already overcrowded lifestyle.

❁ *Apply to your life* ❁

How can we do this? The answer is to stand back, pray for guidance and direction, prune away unnecessary activities, and streamline necessary ones so that we can do what is required for daily life efficiently and work for God effectively.

55 Productive Lives

"Our people must learn to devote themselves to doing what is good, in order that they may provide for daily necessities and not live unproductive lives"

Titus 3:14

Paul is writing to Titus about his travel plans and other practical aspects of life. The good he is urging in this context is not moral, but practical. We can learn a lot by relating to the words he uses. Follow Paul's advice.

Learn For God's sake, I will learn to devote myself to doing what is good. Paul says we need to "learn" to do this. It may not come quickly. I may need to make plans, to read, to practice.

Devote I will devote myself. To "devote" has to do with my attitude. I will make this a priority in my life.

Doing what is good I will do what is good. Making messes is not good. Spending my time unproductively is not good. Making impulsive and poor decisions is not good. Instead, I will decide what is really good for me, for my family and friends, and for the work of the Lord. I will choose a few that I feel God wants me to focus on and set about to accomplish those worthwhile things.

Daily necessities and not unproductive lives Maybe for me, my first priority is to order my house and life in such a way that I will be able to accomplish what is spotlighted in this verse. I will be able to provide for daily necessities and not live an unproductive life.

Disorganized people often have wonderful abilities and accomplish many things in their lives. But how much more could they accomplish of the right things and with so much less stress, if they were working from a well-ordered base?

That's what I want for myself, a live productive for God.

❧ *Apply to your life* ☙

Align your life -- decisions, attitudes, and goals -- with what God wants for you so that you may live your most productive life.

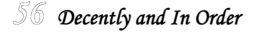

56 Decently and In Order

"Let all things be done properly and in an orderly manner."

1 Corinthians 14:40.

Paul is instructing the church in Corinth about how to hold worship services. Apparently, they had not decided on an orderly procedure so Paul told them what to do to avoid disorder and confusion during the services.

In doing so he leaves us two organizational concepts to consider:

+ properly

+ in an orderly manner

"Properly" means "well, rightly, suitably, appropriately." Do you do things in a proper way, an appropriate way, not just a haphazard or last minute way?

"In an orderly manner" tells us that there are logical steps that will get us most efficiently to our goal. What that way is will vary from one circumstance to another but this verse tell us to avoid doing things carelessly, sloppily, or without attention.

Note that it does not mean "perfectly." There is no perfect organizational method or system. We set reasonable goals and seek to meet those goals in the best way we can. Later, when we have given it thought, we may adjust our system to make it better. Planning carefully and adjusting when we see a more

125

effective way to get things done efficiently will be our way of doing things "properly and in an orderly manner."

❦ *Apply to your life* ❧

Seek a workable plan and work it into your life consistently.

Be alert to needs and solutions.

Set do-able goals and seek them step by step.

57 A Worry Free Life

"When you lie down, your sleep will be sweet"

Proverbs 3:24

"My son, (of course, this applies to daughters as well) preserve sound judgment and discernment and do not let them out of our sight; they will be life for you, an ornament to grace your neck...when you lie down, your sleep will be sweet." (Proverbs 3:21-24)

The young men in Solomon's day lived in a certain sense of moral danger. Not unlike young men of today. If they weren't careful, they could get themselves into a lot of trouble. So Solomon urges them to hang tight to judgment and discernment. Watch that decision making!

There is a way of life for those who follow God's leading that has a certain sense of stability and grace about it. By not letting sound judgment and discernment out of our sights, not just about moral issues, we can step into a way of life in which we can live comfortably and well, not just for ourselves --- though that is important--- but for our families and others whom God brings into our lives.

If we are careless and break all the rules for organizing our time, our living space, our money and whatever else in our lives needs management, we will find ourselves in trouble of a different sort than Solomon's sons. We will be harried and stressed. We won't be able to find things easily, know certainly when and where our appointments are, and be prepared for unexpected company. We will lack what Solomon elegantly calls "an ornament to grace your neck." Our sleep will not be the sweet sleep which comes when our lives are working right and are consistently under control.

Sound judgment and discernment applies when we choose our activities, when we decide what to keep and what to get rid of, when we work on good habits of tidiness and when we set up a routine of maintenance. Without them, life will unravel and, without Solomon's reminder, we might never have known what went wrong.

☙ *Apply to your life* ❧

Have you been living carelessly in relations to your decisions and choices?

When you go to bed at night, are you satisfied with what you have gotten done that day and the way you are living your life?

58 Twiddling Modern Style

Don't twiddle your thumbs.

Proverbs 6:6-11 CEV

People don't twiddle their thumbs much any more. Maybe they never did. But we all know that it means a person sits around doing nothing. This verse has various translations and renderings in other versions:

"How long will you lie down, O sluggard?" asks the King James Version. The Message by Eugene Peterson renders it, "So how long are you going to laze around doing nothing?"

We like to cut ourselves slack by making excuses for not working as hard as we should. Many are legitimate. But we should always ask ourselves if we are doing as well as we could in the light of what needs to be done.

King Solomon offers a concrete example. He tells us to watch the hard working ant that TOILS to be sure to have enough food for the winter. It not only works to eat today. Its little insect mind somehow anticipates its future needs.

Then King Solomon gets really practical. Don't sit around when there is a pressing need to get busy. Don't take too many days off work. Don't spend too much time in bed at night or taking naps. In our day he would have mentioned spending too much time watching TV, playing video games, or browsing the internet. These things creep into our lives.

There is a time and place for all these things. But the warning is there. If you take it easy when you should be working, you will end up in need like the man in the chapter before this one. He bemoans his undisciplined and misspent life. He gets to the end and has nothing to show for it. O how he regrets it! (Proverbs 5:12-14) I guess he did too much twiddling.

○ぴ *Apply to your life* ♂○

Are you participating in too much rest, TV, or other recreation into your life when you should be working?

Are you making wise plans for the future by consulting financial advisors?

Can you think of anything else you need to be doing to prepare for the future, especially concerning retirement income?

Entertain Angels and Others

"Be not forgetful to entertain strangers for thereby some have entertained angels unawares."

Hebrews 13:2

Usually the people we entertain are not angels, not the usual kind anyway. They are Uncle Fred and Aunt Alice with their kids who have dropped by on their way to Florida or some of the ladies from the church women's ministry who are meeting to plan next year's agenda. Another version translates this verse as "show hospitality."

In Bible times there were no Holiday Inns or restaurant franchises so people who were away from their homes were more dependent on others for their needs. Sometimes they were unexpected guests as was the case when Abraham's unexpected visitors (who were angels, by the way) came for dinner. Sometimes they were traveling evangelists and missionaries passing through. And sometimes they were men of God who could count on a place to stay when they were in the area as Elisha did in his special guest room provided by the well-to-do woman. (2 Kings 4:10)

Unexpected guests who drop in, a last minute invitation to visitors to come home for Sunday dinner, or house guests, all require different kinds of preparation. Some of us have a special gift of hospitality. Others of us simply do our best to follow the admonition which lingers for all to obey, "Forget not to show hospitality." This takes being organized.

If we are open to it, undoubtedly many visitors, angels or not, will bring messages of various kinds from God. Who knows, maybe sometimes one of those messengers will be the real thing?

ℭ *Apply to your life* ℬ

Are your public rooms generally ready for visitors?

Is your mind and attitude generally ready for them?

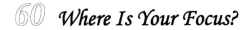

60 Where Is Your Focus?

"Set your minds on things above, not on earthly things."

Colossians 3:2

Unlike those lizards with bulgy eyes that can rotate independently in different directions, humans are limited to looking in only one direction at a time. Our minds are that way, too. We can either focus on "things above" or on "earthly things." Not both at once.

The Bible speaks of this contrast often. In Psalm 17:14 David lists scathing indictments against his enemies. As he ticks off their characteristics he states that their "portion is in this life."

By contrast in the next verse he tells where his own heart is. "As for me, I shall behold Thy face in righteousness; I will be satisfied with Thy likeness when I awake." (NASV)

Obviously this does not mean that we don't think about our earthly responsibilities to set up our homes properly, decorate, and streamline our use of time. It does mean that our priority is not in that area. As a matter of fact, one reason we need to organize is so we can shift our attention to more important things than this life only.

James uses the term a "double-minded man."(James 1:8) In our context, a double-minded person would be one who keeps shifting his focus from "things above" to "earthly things."

Our hearts and minds unclench our fist from the things we have on this earth. Be grateful for them, sure, and use them in a responsible way. But keep in mind we have a higher calling to God's kingdom, to draw our satisfaction from our personal relation with God and to take advantage our opportunities to serve him here in this life.

❧ *Apply to your life* ☙

Let go of any hold that earthly things have on your mind and heart. More importantly, set your mind on things above. Then work out that focus in your life.

61 *Finish What You Start*

"So here's what I think: The best thing you can do right now is to finish what you started last year and not let those good intentions grow stale. Your heart's been in the right place all along. You've got what it takes to finish up, so go to it. Once the commitment is clear, you do what you can, not what you can't."

2 Corinthians 8:9ff (The Message)

In the middle of the book of 2 Corinthians where Paul speaks of many important and lofty truths, he turns to the idea of giving. It is a lofty idea in itself, bridging spiritual commitment and practicality. Paul gives very sound advice concerning the offering they had planned to make. We might call it a pep talk.

Do you have a project you have started? Or one you should have started? Are your intentions in danger of going stale?

The words of Paul nudge us to do the right thing.

- ◆ Your heart is in the right place.

- ◆ You've got what it takes to finish up.

- ◆ The commitment is clear.

- ◆ Do what you can.

❦ *Apply to your life* ❧

Name a project that you need to do, something you feel God wants you to do whether of a "spiritual" or "practical" nature.

Take Paul's admonition to heart. Write it down.

Write a few steps.

Renew your commitment and then, as Paul says, "go to it."

# 62 *Give Careful Thought*

"Give careful thought to your ways,"

Haggai 1:7

"Give careful thought to your ways" says the Lord to those who were working hard to get things back in shape after their seventy year absence from the Promised Land. The problem was that they had developed tunnel vision. All they worked on was their own houses. They had not begun to build the house of the Lord.

God points this out to them and says again, "Give careful thought to your ways." He points out that "My house ... remains a ruin while each of you is busy with his own house."

One of the reasons Christians want so desperately to get their houses organized is so that it will not be a distraction to the higher calling of doing God's work.

Sure, it was important for them to build a home to get out of the rain and heat when they returned to the Promised Land. That was not the problem. The problem was that they got so caught up in their own affairs, they forgot God's. There comes a time when it is time to move on.

It comes down to a matter of priorities and balance. Let's get our launching pad, our home, organized. Let's get a system that makes life work efficiently. Then we can turn our thoughts elsewhere. "Give careful thought to your ways," and never lose sight of God's purpose in the world.

☙ *Apply to your life* ❧

Do you have the proper balance between meeting your daily needs and doing the work God has for you?

Think about it -- carefully.

God Loves to Organize

"God called the light Day and the darkness he called Night."

Genesis 1:4, 5

God left us the pattern for how to organize. "God divided the light from the darkness". Then he labeled what he had separated. The first chapter of Genesis states repeatedly that God grouped things that are alike together on various days and separated their creation into different days.

When the children of Israel traveled, they did so in groups of each tribe and each tribe had its specific place to locate when they set up camp. When they went into the Promised Land, each tribe was separate from the other and God told each tribe where they were to locate.

Sorting into similar groups is the basic mechanism for creating order. We sort things together that are going to be used together.

We upgrade the efficiency of our house by tightening our commitment to putting things that are alike into one spot. Some examples from my house are:

Photography items (cameras, film, batteries)

Repair supplies (several kinds of glue, wire, duct tape)

Shoe stuff (polish, shoe strings, brushes)

Work tools (hammers, screw drivers, nails and screws)

Hair products (shampoo, conditioner, hair color - Oops! I guess the secret is out about that now)

Cleaning products (window spray ...Well, you get the idea about how it works.)

Once you gather your household items together, you will see how much you have and what size container you need to hold them. Locate the appropriate size box, basket, drawer, or whatever it takes to make sure those items stay together. Put often used items in an easy to reach place. Place less often used items in a less accessible place if space is limited.

"God called the light Day and the darkness he called Night." Just as God put a name to what he did, we need to label our groupings with a name. Attach a label, usually a three by five card with the name of the grouping on it, to the box or basket so that the contents of the box have an official designation. That final step works wonders in maintaining the organization you have set up.

Keeping things in a jumble doesn't work. Storing things that are alike together is the only way we can function efficiently.

❧ *Apply to your life* ☙

Try to group things together wherever possible. You'll find it is a very ancient approach that is very powerful.

64 Never Too Busy

"But a certain Samaritan, as he journeyed, came where he was, and when he saw him, he had compassion."

Luke 10:23

We emphasize scheduling and keeping on task because our tendency is to drift into unimportant activities and fritter away our time. But we should never be so rigid in our schedule that we fail to stop to meet the important needs of others.

The priest and the Levite kept to their agendas and ignored the poor guy lying in the ditch. But the Samaritan was willing to set aside his own schedule to step up to the plate when an unexpected and important need arose.

Should we stop for every little need someone else brings to us? Certainly not. But neither should we isolate ourselves from the unexpected and legitimate needs of others.

Helping others in need *is* one of our priorities. Notice that he had his money and was prepared to help. Notice too that he took time to help the man adequately but then went on with his schedule. We need to be organized so that we can help on the spur of the moment.

We call him The Good Samaritan, and so he was. But he was prepared to do good because he was prepared and organized.

❦ *Apply to your life* ❧

Is your heart open to helping the needy?

What can you do to be more prepared for service?

 Two Household Helpers

"Let us come boldly to the throne of grace that we may obtain mercy and grace to help in time of need"

Hebrews 4:16

It may be difficult for those who do not struggle with disorder to realize how hard it is for those of us who do. They think it is easy just to set aside time to organize and then just do it. For whatever reason, it is not easy for us. We want to change but it is a problem.

Include God in your struggle. Ask him to enable you to live a full life, free of the hindrance of disorganization that hinders you in so many ways. God is interested in all of our needs, big or little. For us, this need is big.

Ask daily for his strength and wisdom to know what to do and then, the power to do it. Pray over your weaknesses, tendencies that you know keep you in bondage. Ask for God's help in changing your attitudes, thoughts, and behaviors, not necessarily in that order.

Sometimes the conduct changes come first because, whether we want to or not, we can change our behavior by an act of the will. But it takes God's sending his handmaidens, Mercy and Grace.

I need all the household help I can get. I would welcome two hardworking young ladies named Mercy and Grace if they knocked on my front door. However, I doubt they will come in flesh and blood form.

Perhaps they will be even more help in their spiritual form as they flow from the throne of God.

❀ *Apply to your life* ❀

Don't try to do it alone.

God has help available for the asking.

Zealous of Good Works

"That he might redeem us from all iniquity and purify unto himself a people of his own, zealous of good works."

Titus 2:14b

The Bible speaks of "good work" and "good works" of Christians at least twenty-eight times.

A few fragments of these verses are these:

- "That they may see your good works" Matthew 5:16

- "Be adorned with good works" 1 Timothy 2:10

- "That they may be rich in good works" 1 Timothy 6:18

- "Furnished to all good works" 2 Timothy 3:17

- "Careful to maintain good works" Titus 3:8

- "Provoke to love and good works" Hebrews 10:24

- "By good works glorify God" 1 Peter 2:12

There are many more like these. These clear admonitions are more remarkable when we realize that these people lived in a world without modern conveniences (come to think of it, that more simple way of life may have been a benefit) In addition, they were struggling with being persecuted as Christians.

Though they are not a requirement for salvation (Ephesians 2:8), good works are so bound up in the

Christian life that they were expected under all circumstances (Ephesians 2:9).

What has all of this got to do with being organized? Just this: a disorganized person often can't get their act together to take care of themselves, much less to help others. Disorganization cuts the heart out of productivity.

You want to send a book to an unsaved friend but you lose the address (or the book). You are late to teaching your Sunday school class because your Sunday morning routine was not streamlined. You want to make cookies for someone in need but don't have all the ingredients. You can't open your home for hospitality to the lost and the brethren because ... well, you know why.

On and on it goes. In a myriad of little ways, disorder causes us to stumble in doing work God has for us to do.

❤ *Apply to your life* ❤

We can't do every good work we see needs doing. But we can do our part --- if we are organized to do so.

67 *Lack Wisdom?*

"If any of you lack wisdom, let him ask of God."

James 1:5

As we look at our lives and the lives of many others, we see the need for wisdom in knowing how to balance our lives.

Are we trying to cram too many activities into our lives; too many belongings?

Are we doing too little, experiencing lethargy, ennui? We just let too much slide?

When we plan and actually get down to working on a project, are we working on the right thing, the thing that will really make a difference in your life and the lives of others?

Someone has said that if the devil can't keep us from getting on the horse he will flip us off the other side. It is easy to become unbalanced in what we do and how we do it.

But we are not left there. "Let him ask of God," says James. In this case, James was addressing the problem of suffering and saying that God will show the church the value of persecution it was going through.

Though housekeeping is not smack dab in the middle of spiritual warfare like suffering is, for some of us doing what we ought in this area is a significant part of our spiritual struggle. We need to ask God for wisdom on how to go about our daily lives in a way that is pleasing to him.

Undoubtedly we will not hear a voice from above saying, "Vacuum the living room," "Empty the dishwasher," or "Pick up the toys." We will find, however, a lot of guidance on living lives of order and simplicity. The book of Proverbs, the last chapters of Ephesians and Colossians, and sprinkled all throughout the Bible are instructions on where our emphasis in life should be. From those we evaluate what we need to do and how we do it. Then we adjust ourselves to a wise way of life instructed by the Bible and empowered by the Holy Spirit.

☙ *Apply to your life* ❧

Let's face it. Some of us have organizing skills naturally. Others don't. Those in the second category have every reason to ask for what we need in this area.

Go to the Ant

Go to the ant, you sluggard; consider its ways and be wise! It has no commander, no overseer or ruler, yet it stores its provisions in summer and gathers its food at harvest.

How long will you lie there, you sluggard? When will you get up from your sleep? A little sleep, a little slumber, a little folding of the hands to rest---and poverty will come on you like a bandit and scarcity like an armed man.

Proverbs 6: 6-11

Wow, this looks like tough guy talk. And indeed it is! As women we probably would not be as straightforward as King Solomon was in giving his advice. We would probably say gently, "Honey, don't you think you should spend less time on the sofa looking at television? You know the house is not going to pick itself up or clean itself."

You don't have a supervisor or boss to stand over you so you need to take your own initiative. Look around at how things work in life. Any time things get done, even in nature, it is because somebody is doing a lot of work.

You think that if you slack off a little here and a little there it won't matter but it all adds up. After a while you will look around and be amazed at how messy things have gotten. It works the other way as well. If you keep doing a little here and there consistently, you will be amazed at how much will get done and how good your house will look.

If you don't get up and get going, not only now but on a regular basis, this place is going to be a wreck not only now but as a regular thing.

However, you say it; whether tough like Solomon or gently as in my advice to "Honey", the truth is the same. Work pays off and failing to work brings big-time problems. Having said that, I have to hop up myself and get moving to keep this house under control.

❦ *Apply to your life* ❧

Take Solomon's advice to heart. Make work a priority. The Lord just may have this message for you.

 # *Watch Us Go!*

"Loose him and let him go"

John 11:44

What words of power! Lazarus had been dead. He had been resurrected by the "Lazarus come forth" words of Jesus. But he was not yet fully free. He was still entangled in grave clothes from which he had yet to be removed.

So it is with many of us in many of life's struggles. We are becoming alive, but are not yet fully free to move about our lives without encumbrances. For us clutter and disorganization are one of those hindrances from which we need to be extricated.

But how? Jesus told others to lose Lazarus from his bonds. Though we can find help from others with the mess sitting around the house, unfortunately, no one but us can touch the entanglements within ourselves which keep us from living fully free. Without inner freedom we will return to the thoughts and feelings which drive us to keep too much, leave out too much, and procrastinate too much.

Sometimes, in a moment of enlightenment, we say to ourselves, "I am crazy! I am really insane to live this way! God has another, more wonderful way of life for me. I will enter into his freedom." In those moments, large chunks of grave clothes drop releasing us from the urge to clutter. Other pieces follow soon.

For some of us it release comes more slowly. Those grave clothes stick mighty close for a long time.

Slowly, by an act of the will prompted by God's spirit, we pick away one little piece at a time. Release comes at a snail's pace. But it comes.

For those who are alive in Christ, the possibility of freedom, even from the messy lifestyle which has hindered our fullest living, the words "Loose him and let him go!" are a clarion call of hope. "Yes, Lord, loose us and watch us go! Oh, watch us go!"

❈ *Apply to your life* ❈

Do you ever feel hampered by clutter and disorganization?

What word or words would express your feelings if you could be finally free of the thoughts and habits that keep you bound?

70 *Love Not the World*

"Love not the world, neither the things that are in the world. If any man love the world, the love of the Father is not in him."

1 John 2:15

"Set your affections on things above."

Colossians 3:2

Notice the words, "the things that are in the world." For us, these things are probably not evil influences centered in the world. They are the items of every day life which somehow, like a strangler fig tree, have wrapped themselves around our hearts.

The admonition not to love the things that are in the world strikes at the heart of a problem many of us have, the tendency to keep too much of the world's goods. Speaking of his mother who hoarded many items, a friend of mine said, "These things are her friends. She loves them." Many of the goods we gather around us act as our friends. They bring us comfort. We love them.

And yet, though John tells us not to go that route with our affections, the fists of our souls hold goods tightly. We fear to let them go. We hate to let them go. It is an emotional thing. And yet we are told not to love them.

We have focused our thoughts on the things of the world. But the power of the verse is in the words, "the love of the Father is not in him." Could it be that the love of God and the love of these things displace each other?

Am I willing to let go of:

- too many books for the space I have;

- activities and hobbies that take up too much time and energy;

- duplicates of tools, office supplies, and other products;

- too many hours spent on the job;

- or whatever it is that has an unholy grasp of my life?

These things are not bad in themselves. But if we can't let them go even when they interfere with living our lives productively for God, we love them too much and God too little.

❧ Apply to your life ☙

Concentrate on your devotion to God and the importance of that. Perhaps the things of life will grow strangely dim in the light of his glory and grace.

71 *Organizing as Devotion*

"Neither will I offer burnt offerings unto the lord my God of that which doth cost me nothing."

2 Samuel 24:24

Someone had offered to give David everything he needed in order to make a sacrifice to God. But deep in his heart David recognized that worship demanded personal involvement on his part. He would not accept the gift and take the easy way out. He insisted on paying for what he needed.

One morning I looked at a jumbled bookcase. I had avoided tackling the mess and, as with all messes, I was suffering from living with it. Still, I procrastinated because it seemed like a big, ugly job. I had no heart for it.

One morning after my morning time with God, a new thought occurred to me. "I can do it for the Lord! Perhaps it would make him happy to know this is an act of worship to him."

The distasteful job took on a different aura. It was my pleasure to create something nice for him. My movements were dedicated to him. My bookcase became a little altar and my "sacrifice," small in some ways but large in others, was the neatness created in that bookcase.

We are not required to be neat in order to be accepted nor would I suggest for a moment that cleanliness is next to godliness. It is not wise to equate all of our housework with worship. Then every undone housekeeping job becomes a spiritual condemnation. Many a disorganized housekeeper has communed with her Maker in the midst of clutter.

On the other hand, as the Spirit moves us to see, one little unkempt table, a small cluttered corner, or maybe a needy refrigerator can become an opportunity for worship.

It did cost me something to arrange that book case. But it was a price I was very glad to pay.

○ʒ *Apply to your life* ♋

Can you find a spot in your life where you can worship God with your service?

72 *Power to Act*

"Do not withhold good from those who deserve it,
when it is in your power to act"

Proverbs 3:27

We are on earth for several purposes. One of them is to do good for others. A good reason for making sure our lives are strong and well ordered is so we can help people who deserve it. Sometimes we are prospering them on their way as when we entertain and support missionaries. Sometimes we help people get out of trouble if that help is appropriate.

I like the statement about "those who deserve it." We are not responsible to run around throwing good works at every real or perceived need. *Who* to help requires some judgment on our part. It is not a question of whether the person is good enough for our help. The question is in two parts:

* In our best judgment, will our help be beneficial to the person and circumstances? This is not always easy to ascertain because some problems are so chronic and convoluted that we might make it worse if we are not careful. Often it is best to volunteer to work with an organization that has experience in the best ways to offer assistance.

* In our best judgment, are we in a position to offer help, that is, are we in a position to act? Would it be wise for us to move in this way?

However, the general rule is this: offer help when you are able. Our responsibility is to make sure we are in a position of power so we can help when we need to. For many of us that means the house must be good enough to have folks in, often unexpectedly. Sometimes it means having house guests. It means you can give someone a ride because you are not ashamed of the trash in the car. It means being able to volunteer because you don't feel you have to stay home and clean.

There are many aspects of power to help. Being organized enough to help is one of them.

❦ *Apply to your life* ❧

Is there somebody in your life who deserves your help?

Do you have the power to help it?

Should you?

73 Being Pruned Is No Fun

*"Walk worthy of the Lord unto all pleasing, being
fruitful in every good work."*

Colossians 1:10

"Ouch! Oh! Hey! Whoa! Stop!" These are the
words you might hear from an apple tree, or any plant
for that matter, as its owner prunes its branches.
Sometimes the branches are dead and unproductive.
Sometimes there are too many branches and even the
good ones need to be pruned. If branches are allowed
to grow untended, eventually the tree will fail to
produce apples for the owner.

Isn't that the way it is with us.

Sometimes God wants to prune away destructive
and hurtful things in our lives so we will be more
productive. In our homes, desire to keep too much stuff
and habits which lead to clutter need to be pruned
away. "Ouch! Oh!" It hurts to give up our "precious
treasures" that, in reality are clutter keeping us from
being the tree God wants us to be.

Sometimes God prunes away perfectly fine
activities. We have too many of them. "Hey! Whoa!
Those are good activities. I don't want to give them
up!" Too many activities are sucking the life from fruit
production. We have a lot of fine foliage. We may
even make a fine appearance. But a closer look reveals
we have not produced fruit.

"Help!" In our lives, often we must prune
ourselves. That reality is really hard. It hurts to get rid

of clutter we think we must keep in order to be happy. We feel pain when we give up good activities that are just not appropriate for us at this time. But pruning is a Biblical reality.

ɔ৪ *Apply to your life* ৪ɔ

What are you willing to prune from your life? Clutter? Habits? Activities?

Be specific about which ones need to go in order to "walk worthy of the Lord unto all pleasing, being fruitful in every good work." (Colossians 1:10)

74 Growing Up

"I put away childish things."

1 Corinthians 13:11

There is winsomeness in the personality of someone who carries some of the characteristics of childhood into adult life. Those who are spontaneous, who live happily in the moment, and who are guileless and open are enjoyable to be with. Reflecting this, Jesus admonished his followers to have sincere faith like little children when he said, "Whosoever shall not receive the kingdom of God as a little child; he shall not enter therein." Mark 10:15 (KJV)

However, there are times when we should not act like children. The apostle Paul wrote of his experience in this regard when he said "When I was a child, I spake as a child, I understood as a child, I thought as a child: but when I became a man (an adult), I put away childish things." (1 Corinthian 13:11 KJV)

In our case, one of the reasons we accumulate clutter is because we cling to inappropriate thoughts and feelings which should be changed.

- We "love" our belongings as a child loves his teddy or blankie.

- We fear danger so we keep many protections such as unnecessary papers we are afraid we will need later.

- We make decisions based on feeling, not on sensible responsibility. So we do something fun

- instead of what we know we need to and should do.

- We hope and dream some force outside ourselves will solve our problem instead of realizing the buck has appropriately stopped at our desk.

These characteristics don't fly any more in the adult world. We have the responsibility and fortunately, the power to create an orderly and beautiful environment. But maturity doesn't happen automatically. As we mature, like Paul we make one decision after another to "put away childish things."

⊂ঙ *Apply to your life* ৵⊃

Move into adult responsibility one step at a time. Can you identify one inappropriate childlike area in your life today?

Then, make an adult decision about how to "put it away" or out of your adult life.

One adult decision after another will add up to a life of satisfying maturity.

Seed Sown Among Thorns

"Still others, like seed sown among thorns, hear the word, but the worries of this life , the deceitfulness of wealth and the desires for other things come in, and choke the work, making it unfruitful"

Mark 4:19

God is sowing seeds in your heart. He wants them to grow and bring forth a lot of fruit. Only you can say what those seeds might be. Only you can say what fruit God (and you as his child) want to see in your life. The likelihood is that they fall into three categories.

- *Seeds in your personal life.* How are you doing personally in relation to things only you know about? Are some of those seeds struggling? Are you frustrated in relation to your time and condition of the house? Are you emotionally whipped? Are you spiritually sluggish? Or are those seeds and others growing vigorously in your personal life in many areas?

- *Seeds in your family and social life.* Is your family life working smoothly? Do you feel that you are fulfilling God's will in relation to your family and social life?

- *Seeds in your service for the Lord.* Are you able to serve the Lord with vigor and enthusiasm? Are you reaching out with the message of hope and salvation?

God wants the seeds of his word sown in our hearts to grow energetically; especially the words of salvation. However many things can interfere with that growth. Growth is sapped by "the worries of this life, the deceitfulness of wealth and the desires for other things." Ah, as Wordsworth said, "The world is too much with us."

❧ *Apply to your life* ☙

Here is my warning

Pull up weeds that stunt growth.

Abandon preoccupation with possessions.

Here is my encouragement

Seeds are designed to grow. Once those weeds have been uprooted, you will bloom and produce good things for God.

76 *Wisdom's House*

"Wisdom has built her house..."

Proverbs 9:1

The passage goes on to describe how the woman described as Wisdom has worked to prepare her house and direct her maids in order to prepare for a party to which she invites others. She wants to edify her guests with instructions in how to "walk in the way of understanding."

"The woman Folly is loud; she is undisciplined and without knowledge..."

Proverbs 9:19

She too is having a get-together for which she makes little preparation. She sits in her doorway and calls to her guests to come and learn how to live foolishly.

Although these are metaphors, they remind us that we, as housekeepers, have a choice. Like wisdom, we can be wise and do it right which includes planning, work, and supervision of others. Or, like Folly, we can go about it in an undisciplined way and be ill prepared for the party of life.

Wisdom and Folly apply to many areas of life but with our focus on homebuilding, we can easily see that if we want to be successful we need to be the woman who plans and works hard.

We need to set wise priorities, learn how to do the job, make plans for their execution, and work hard in carrying them out. Boy! Would that make a change in the house!

Let's avoid keeping company with Folly who doesn't know how to do the job and what's more, does not have the discipline to do it even if she knew how.

All of us know that approach won't take long to show itself in the living room, bathroom, bedroom --- well, you know --- everywhere!

❈ *Apply to your life* ❧

In your life, what is Wisdom?

What is Folly?

77 *Thinking Ahead*

"Suddenly I realized that others would someday get everything I had worked for so hard, and then I started hating it all. Who knows if those people will be sensible or stupid? Either way, they will own everything I have earned by hard work and wisdom. It doesn't make sense. I thought about all my hard work and I felt depressed."

Ecclesiastes 2:18-20 CEV

The book of Ecclesiastes is a search for meaning in life. One of the issues dealt with is the problem of what happens to all of our things when we die. In Solomon's case, he had accumulated a lot of things his children wanted to inherit.

As you look around, what do you have to leave that your family will really want? And what, as is often the case, are things that are meaningful only to you and will cause a major headache to you or anybody else when time comes to dispose of your belongings?

How many times has family planned to hold an estate sale and then had to wade through piles of useless and meaningless stuff? The items that the owner struggled to get and keep then become a burden to others.

There may be valuable and useful furniture. There may be precious pieces of jewelry as well. While the furniture is easy to find but sometimes the jewelry pieces may be overlooked or lost in the clutter.

But the big problem is often papers. What seemed like valuable information to the owner becomes trash to those whose job it is to handle it. Again, valuable papers and information may become lost in the abundance of unimportant papers.

Some things are useful to keep for yourself even if they may not be meaningful to your family. But maybe a lot of what you have is really unnecessary and causes more problem in your life than it is worth.

❈ *Apply to your life* ❈

Are there unnecessary things that are obscuring valuables?

Do you need to pare down what you have, both for now and the future?

Do you need to take control of your paperwork, filing and storing in such a way that you and others can find your important papers?

Do you need to call in a professional organizer or other help with the organizing that needs to be done?

78 Watch for the Crown of Goodness

"Thou crownest the year with thy goodness."

Psalm 65:11

There is a great big wonderful world out there for us to enjoy. It is easy to forget this when we are concentrating on changing our house and behavior. Our focus becomes overcoming obstacles instead enjoying of the wonder of life.

Lift your eyes beyond difficulties or struggles. Keep in mind that God has blessed us with much. Even our problem with clutter often reflects the abundance available to us in our world. Our issues with time management are evidence of all of the good opportunities in our life. We just need to manage all of this blessing. Try limiting opportunities or eliminating some of the abundance.

In Psalm 65, David revels in the beauty and power of nature - mountains, crashing waves, sunsets and sunrises (vs. 6-8). Then he talks about the overflow of agriculture as God blesses with crops and livestock (vs. 9-13). His greatest rejoicing is in God's spiritual gifts (vs. 1-5).

Certainly we are working to improve our way of life. We want to organize our homes, streamline our time management, manage our finances and taxes, train our children, and a hundred other things necessary for order and serenity in our lives. But as we struggle in some areas to make progress or overcome disorganization in our homes and lives, we would be shortsighted if we didn't lift our eyes to things beyond the mundane.

Remember there is a wonder and joy to life. Continue the journey with enthusiasm. If things of this world are hindering us from enjoying the goodness of God then our mission is clear. Move forward vigorously to overcome them. Then we can step more and more completely into the fullness of the good things with which God has crowned our world.

ෲ *Apply to your life* ෬

Be alert and grateful for the things around you. Step into the wonder and wildness of God's world around you. It will strengthen your soul for the work you are doing in other areas of your life.

*"I would not have come to know sin except through the
Law, for I would not have known about coveting if the
Law had not said, "YOU SHALL NOT COVET."*

Romans 7:7

Paul was going along, trying to live a godly life
(doing a pretty good job of it in his way of thinking)
when he was caught short by the command, "YOU
SHALL NOT COVET."

In the next verse he confesses he was then troubled
by "coveting of every kind." When Paul "woke up" to
covetousness in his own life, he began to realize just
how very covetous he was. Wow, it was everywhere in
his heart and mind!

That is the way our awareness works. Once we buy
a green car, we suddenly become aware of how many
green cars there are on the road. A growing awareness
of coveting works that way as well.

Webster's New Collegiate Dictionary gives a
definition of covetousness as "having a craving for
possessions." These possessions don't have to belong
to somebody else in order to qualify as objects of
covetousness.

Who would have thought that craving things is a
sin? The Bible suggests it is because the things we
crave interfere with our dedication to God. The key
concept is our feelings toward "things," not primarily
how much we have.

- If we crave getting more or keeping too much, we are coveting.

- If we have too much and can't let go, we are coveting.

- If our belongings interfere with our service for God, we are coveting.

- If keeping too much interferes with important relationships and still we won't give up what we have, we are coveting.

These possessions may be good items such as books, potentially valuable collections, memories from the past. They may be good; they are just not good for us in our situation. The key to knowing whether we are coveting is not how much we have but the attitude of heart toward our belongings. If we have a craving for them, a strong inner desire, an inordinate longing, then we, like Paul, need to "fess up" that we have entered into that area of sin called covetousness. And as with all sin, we need to deal with it for what it is --- something God wants us to confess and abandon.

Is it hard? Yes!

Is it impossible? No.

⊂੪ *Apply to your life* ੭⊃

Take a moment to think about the place of "things" in your life. Without minimizing, assess whether your possessions are interfering with your time use, your relationships, your finances, and your service for God.

80 Treasure! Wow!

Sounds Good to Me!

"Lay not up for yourselves treasures upon earth, where moth and rust doth corrupt, and where thieves break through and steal. But lay up for yourselves treasures in heaven where neither moth nor rust doth corrupt and where thieves do not break through nor steal; for where your treasure is, there will your heart be also."

Matthew 6:19-21

Let's tell it like it is. Some of the things we have in our lives really are treasures. Some may indeed have real intrinsic value. But often the real value to us is that they give us comfort. They have put down roots into our hearts and we have become attached. It hurts to remove them --- even to think of removing them.

They may be

- items we have bought because we feel buying quality is the responsible thing to do

- family heirlooms whose main value is nostalgic but may have real worth as well

- irreplaceable antiques

- tools, books, or sports equipment we feel we must have (whether we use them or not)

- gifts from those we love

- items of no value to others that have been left to us by loved ones

Jesus puts his finger on the problem. They are transitory. They can be lost in a calamity like a hurricane, tornado, or earthquake. Jewelry and other valuables can be stolen. Or they can simply deteriorate with time. Some of the things we love will be unappreciated and carelessly disposed of when we are gone. In the long run, they won't mean anything.

Does Jesus mean we should all divest ourselves of homes, carefully purchased furnishings, and inherited items that have been in the family for years? In many cases that would be an unwise and irresponsible thing to do. Though Jesus had no belongings to speak of and no home of his own because of the nature of his mission, in ordinary cases these things are proper for us to have.

As in this case, Jesus often spoke in absolutes to make his point strongly. His statement makes it abundantly clear that we need to evaluate our hearts in relation to getting and keeping belongings.

One test of whether we are in harmony with God's viewpoint about the things we own is whether we are willing to let them go when it is necessary or appropriate to do so. In some cases, it may be easy. More often it hurts to untangle their roots from our hearts. We may feel sorrow to see them go. But if it is somehow in God's will for us at that moment, we can say with a certain amount of submission, "Thy will be done."

Then we need to turn our attention to what is really important, the importance of what will never perish, "buying" eternal treasures for the kingdom of God that will be stored in heaven.

Jesus concludes with the core of his message, "For where your treasure is there will your heart be also." (v. 21)

❧ *Apply to your life* ☙

What valuables are you sending on ahead of you into heaven?

Where is the focus of your love, your heart?

81 Worthless Things

"Turn my eyes away from worthless things; renew my life according to your word."

Psalm 119:37

Eugene Peterson in The Message renders this verse loosely,

"Divert my eyes from toys and trinkets."

Every society experiences problematic trends, emerging issues with which it must deal. In today's world, the overabundance of food and its easy availability has created an epidemic of overweight persons. In the same way, overabundance of products for sale and their easy availability makes it hard not to get and keep too many possessions. We are afflicted with possession obesity.

This verse spotlights this topic, the temptation to focus too much on what this verse calls "worthless things." The writer is probably not talking about buying junk at a yard sale. He means ordinary things that should take a back seat to more important things.

Of course, we need to have a neat and appealing house. We want to look attractive in our clothing and grooming. Our kitchen needs a certain amount of equipment so we can fix meals efficiently. All of these are legitimate things and appropriate for the child of God who lives wisely in the world.

But it is so easy to slip across the line and get caught up in what are sometimes called "the things of this world." They may be good things such as more kitchen equipment, stylish clothes, interesting books, useful electronic equipment, cars, hobbies, and many other things laid out on the beautiful buffet of retail sales we find in a store, catalog, or on the internet. Apparently the writer of this verse felt tempted in this way. He asked God to help him avoid emphasizing things that are in the long run pretty valueless.

How much is too much? Only you can evaluate when things have gone too far in your circumstances. Only you can determine how you are going to solve the problem when meeting legitimate needs morphs into gathering worthless things. One thing we can all do is pray with the psalmist, "Turn my eyes away from worthless things; renew my life according to your word."

❧ *Apply to your life* ☙

Pray for discernment concerning the things of this earth and a renewal of your spiritual life.

82 *Why Was I Born?*

"To this end was I born, and for this cause came I into the world, that I should bear witness unto the truth."

John 18:37

Jesus had a special purpose. He had stepped from eternity in order to become a sacrifice for the sins of the world. These were the words of Jesus as he stood at trial before Pilate. At this moment he made it clear he knew why he had come into the world and he focused on it without wavering.

Jesus is unique. His purpose was unique. However, each of us is here for a purpose of some kind. Esther became queen so she could save the children of Israel from genocide. Jeremiah was told by God that before he was born he was chosen to be a prophet.

This applies to us as well. As Jesus tells his followers, "Ye have not chosen me, but I have chosen you and ordained you that ye should go and bring forth fruit." John.15:16 KJV

If we don't have a sense of calling to an important spiritual work (bearing fruit), our lives will seem very mundane, even purposeless. At different seasons in our lives, the details of how that plays out in our lives varies. In the season of preparation, we may be studying to be ready to serve. Later we may be raising children for the glory of God or caring for elderly relatives. Always in each of these seasons, we need to be spreading God's light to the area we inhabit.

Each of us bears fruit in our own unique way. But one thing seems clear. It is unlikely that any of us is called to spend our time, energy, and focus on baby-sitting clutter or belongings of any kind.

You were born for important work. Do whatever it takes to put unimportant things in the background and your important mission in the foreground so you can fulfill your true destiny.

03 *Apply to your life* 80

What is the focus of this season of your life?

How can you streamline your life to spread God's light as you fulfill your calling during this time?

 *A Simple, Workable Plan*

"When you eat the labor of your hands, you shall be happy, and it shall be well with you."

Psalm 128:2

When we think of our homes and of our dreams for a life of order, beauty, and harmony, we want it to be well with us. God has put in our hearts an irrepressible urge for life. Humans will not tolerate just existence, but seek a life of well being found only by establishing balance. We feel we must get out from under the stress and frustration of the mess we are in. In short, we want to be happy about the surroundings we have created for ourselves and our families.

The secret is in this verse. The psalmist tells us that what we experience comes about by the labor of our hands, our own effort. Nobody else is going to take care of solving our problems for us. That is the well established principle of sowing and reaping. The buck stops with us -- as well it should.

Look at the verse that comes before this one and you will see the background we need for success. Psalm 128:1 says that "how blessed is every one who fears the Lord. Who walks in his ways." Surely, we are not stretching beyond the verse if we conclude that God's way for us is to lead a harmonious and productive life.

Pick out the commands from these two verses. They are simple:

- ◆ Fear the Lord

- Walk in his ways
- Labor with your hands

Now pick out the results:

- We will be blessed
- We will be happy
- It will be well with us

Sounds like a good plan to me.

ℂ℥ *Apply to your life* ℰℨ

This week, using this plan let us get our hearts set on achieving God's way, not only our own. Let us redouble our resolve to work toward the happiness and well being we long for so desperately.

Don't Overdo! Delegate!

Jethro, Moses' father-in-law, scratched his head when he saw Moses working so hard from morning to evening judging the people and asked,

"What are you doing?"

Exodus 18:13-24

Family, even in-laws, can say things to us that others can't. Moses explained to Jethro that he was settling disputes for all of the people of Israel. They stood in line from morning till night to hear his judgment. Jethro was not shy in giving advice. He said:

- "What you are doing is not good."

- "You will only wear yourself out."

- "The work is too heavy for you."

- "You cannot handle it alone."

Then he gave some great advice. Don't keep trying to do it all by yourself. Basically his points were this:

- Pray for the problems of the people.

- Spend your time teaching them. That's your real job.

- Appoint a hierarchy of judges, organize them over various groups.

- You be the supreme judge for only the difficult cases they can't handle.

"That will make your load lighter because they will share it with you." As result you will be "able to stand the strain, and all these people will go home satisfied."

We can't do it all ourselves. We need a team. People in our lives need to be included for their own good as well as for our good.

85 *How to Work Jethro's Plan*

Focus on priorities

- Say NO to less important, C list, priorities.

- Say a resounding YES to a few well selected items in your life.

- List five areas that are priorities in your life, trying to put them in order of importance. Include household maintenance as one of them.

1.

2.

3.

4.

5.

Be efficient

Plan proactively by doing things like the following

- Put dirt catching mats and rugs at entrances to the house to catch the dirt that comes into the house.

- Double up on cooking or put things in the crock pot early in the morning.

- Keep a running list of items you need to buy so you can get them all in one trip.

- Make and use a workable TO-DO list.

- Call for appointments well ahead of time so you can reserve a convenient time.

- Something I can do to be more efficient

_____

Watch the time and plan ahead

- Use one calendar on which all family members write.

- Block out days on the calendar as soon as you know when your vacation time is scheduled at your work, what days the kids are out of school, or any other issues that affect when you can do certain things.

- Record final deadlines for projects.

- Something I can do to plan ahead

_____

Set up a routine

- Set up a cleaning/organizing schedule.

- Set up a meal routine.

- Something I can do to set up a routine

_____

Delegate Don't try to do more jobs than you should.

- Something I can do along this line to do less myself

  _____

- Someone I can hire to help with the housework (or other work)

  _____

- People I can delegate to (either family, friends, or others)

  _____

○ℑ *Apply to your life* ℒ○

Change does not come easily. Take the time to design a plan and then take the time to put it into practice.

 Freedom

"Stand fast in the liberty"

Galatians 1:5

When Paul wrote "Stand fast therefore in the liberty wherewith Christ hath set us free, and be not entangled again with the yoke of bondage," (Galatians 5:1), he was talking about some theological issues that the Galatians were dealing with concerning the topic of salvation.

But I cannot help but think this idea may apply the struggle I have with my house. I feel that I am entangled with a yoke of bondage. For the most part, this yoke is of my own making. I am tangled up with clutter, unproductive habits, ideas that keep leading me back into disorganization.

What do I need to be free from?

- The knee-jerk need to keep anything of "value" that comes into the house.

- Fear of not having enough information (and how much is ever "enough?")

- My own need to take care of others when they can take care of themselves.

- Reluctance to seek professional help for the problems that I think may need help.

If Christ has given me liberty, can I not apply it to these practical things of life? I feel a little like a prisoner who has had the door unlocked but is reluctant to walk out of the cell.

I have only one life here on earth. I want it to be used to its fullest for him. I need to be free to say NO and break free from these destructive thoughts and habits.

Today I will concentrate on my liberty in one area that has entangled me with confusion and disorganization in my life. I will stick with that until it has loosened its hold on me and then go on to another. One step at a time will lead me to freedom from this messy lifestyle.

ᘓ *Apply to your life* ᘔ

What habit, pattern of thought, or piece of clutter will you seek to be free from today?

87 *Higher Ground*

In the words to the hymn, ***Higher Ground***, Johnson Oatman, expresses to the Lord his desire to move forward in his Christian life. He wants to climb out of the valley of Godless living and on a daily basis "scale the utmost height and catch a gleam of glory bright."

The apostle Paul writes about this same journey often in his letters. To Timothy he tells of his own journey from being the chief of sinners to obtaining mercy and being enabled to do the work of spreading the gospel. He says that what happens to him is an example of what can happen to anybody. (1 Timothy 1:12-16)

God is in the changing business. The words of the song and the words penned by Paul are talking about the journey from a life of sin to a life of walking with the Lord. However, those who are making any kind of journey from an undesirable place in life to a better one can relate to the picture they paint.

In our daily organizational lives one of the areas we want to change is to move closer and closer toward a life of harmony. Instead of struggling with clutter, we seek clear surfaces. Instead of keeping too many items, we want to thin them out. Instead of living inefficiently, losing things, procrastinating, and the like, we want to embrace a saner and more orderly way of life. In short, as the hymn states it, we "want to live above the world" as it presents itself to us on a daily basis.

There is a better way of life for each of us. No matter on what level we find ourselves, we all seek to improve and gain new heights of order and beauty in our lives. One foot after another, we scale the heights. If we slip back from time to time as all climbers do, we resume our journey upward toward our goal.

In relation to daily household living, our goal is a noble one. We want to provide a home where our personal needs can be easily met because we have clean clothes, warm beds, and good food on a regular basis. We want our homes to be reasonably stress free. We want to be able to find the items we need to accomplish our jobs. We would like to be able to relate to family and friends in a comfortable way, unencumbered by confusion and clutter.

Our goal is simple. The path to it, however, is not necessarily simple. In a complex world we have to watch the rocks along the way and discern wisely the path to take. But step by step, because God is in the changing business, we can reach higher and higher ground.

ଓ *Apply to your life* ଔ

In your own words, state your thoughts about improving in the area of order and beauty.

Note: The words (and music) to the hymn are easily found using your favorite computer search engine or most hymn books.

Contents by Scripture Reference

The Messies Anonymous Organization

Messies Anonymous is a fellowship of those who struggle with clutter and disorder in their lives. Sometimes Messies work on the program individually using M.A. principles and receiving help from the many books available. Many succeed in this way and find themselves changed and their lives changed from the burden of the messy life-style. Others feel the need to gather together in M.A. groups to find help for their common problem. All of us seek to fulfill the purpose for which we are put on the earth and that is hindered by disorder.

No organizational problem is beyond help. We focus on ourselves and the ways of thinking and feeling that got us into this destructive way of life. As the Messie begins to absorb the program, her life will begin to change slowly but surely. We learn this program by sharing and working the Twelve Steps* as they apply to disorder, not by the traditional educational process. In groups, we tell our stories, our hopes, strengths, fears, and insights into healing.

Whether you seek recovery in a group or individually as you apply the principles of M.A. you will find the beauty, order, and dignity that you seek for your life.

*The Twelve Steps and Twelve Traditions of Messies Anonymous and the Twelve Steps and Traditions of Alcoholics Anonymous, on which they are based, are found on the following pages.

The Twelve Steps of Messies Anonymous

1. We admitted we were powerless over clutter and disorganization-that our lives have become unmanageable.

2. We came to believe that a Power greater than ourselves could restore us to sanity.

3. We made a decision to turn our will and our lives to the care of God as we understood Him.

4 We made a searching and fearless moral inventory of ourselves.

5. We admitted to God, ourselves, and to another human being the exact nature of our wrongs.

6. We are entirely ready to have God remove all these defects in character.

7. We humbly asked Him to remove our shortcomings.

8. We made a list of all persons we had harmed, and became willing to make amends to them all.

9. We make direct amends to such people whenever possible, except when to do so would injure or harm others.

10. We continue to take personal inventory, and when we were wrong promptly admitted it.

11. We sought Him through prayer and meditation to improve our conscious contact with God as we understood Him, praying only for the knowledge of His will for us and power to carry that out.

12. Having had a spiritual awakening as the result of these steps, we tried to carry this message to others who suffer from disorganization in their lives, and to practice these principles in all our affairs.

The Twelve Traditions of Messies Anonymous

1. Our common welfare should come first; personal progress depends on group unity.

2. For our group purpose there is but one ultimate authority - a loving Higher Power. Our leaders are but trusted servants, they do not govern.

3. The only requirement for membership in a MA group is freedom from clutter and a disorganized lifestyle. Any such group may call itself a Messies Anonymous group provided that, as a group, they have no other affiliation.

4. Each group should be autonomous except when action taken would be inconsistent with program principles and guidelines, as described in M.A. literature.

5. Each group has but one primary purpose - to HELP those who desire a sanely organized lifestyle.

6. An MA group ought never endorse, finance, or lend the MA name to any outside property, lest problems of money, property and prestige divert us from our primary purpose.

7. Every MA group ought to be self-supporting declining outside contributions.

8. MA should never remain forever nonprofessional, but our service center workers may employ special workers.

9. MA as such ought never be organized: but we may create service boards or committees directly responsible to those they serve.

10. MA has no opinion on outside issues: hence the MA name ought never to be drawn into public controversy.

11. Our public relations policy is based on attraction rather than promotion: we always maintain person anonymity at the level of press, television, radio, and films.

12. Anonymity is the spiritual foundation of all our traditions, ever reminding us to place principles over personalities.

The Twelve Steps of Alcoholics Anonymous

1. We admitted we were powerless over alcohol— that our lives had become unmanageable.

2. Came to believe that a Power greater than ourselves could restore us to sanity.

3. Made a decision to turn our will and our lives over to the care of God as we understood Him.

4. Made a searching and fearless moral inventory of ourselves.

5. Admitted to God, to ourselves, and to another human being the exact nature of our wrongs.

6. Were entirely ready to have God remove all these defects of character.

7. Humbly asked Him to remove our shortcomings.

8. Made a list of all persons we had harmed, and became willing to make amends to them all.

9. Made direct amends to such people wherever possible, except when to do so would injure them or others.

10. Continued to take personal inventory and when we were wrong promptly admitted it.

11. Sought through prayer and meditation to improve our conscious contact with God, as we understood Him, praying only for knowledge of His will for us and the power to carry that out.

12. Having had a spiritual awakening as the result of these Steps, we tried to carry this message to alcoholics, and to practice these principles in all our affairs.

The Twelve Traditions of Alcoholics Anonymous

1. Our common welfare should come first; personal recovery depends upon A.A. unity.

2. For our group purpose there is but one ultimate authority — a loving God as He may express Himself in our group conscience.
Our leaders are but trusted servants; they do not govern.

3. The only requirement for A.A. membership is a desire to stop drinking.

4. Each group should be autonomous except in matters affecting other groups or A.A. as a whole.

5. Each group has but one primary purpose — to carry its message to the alcoholic who still suffers.

6. An A.A. group ought never endorse, finance, or lend the A.A. name to any related facility or outside enterprise, lest problems of money, property, and prestige divert us from our primary purpose.

7. Every A.A. group ought to be fully self-supporting, declining outside contributions.

8. Alcoholics Anonymous should remain forever non-professional, but our service centers may employ special workers.

9. A.A., as such, ought never be organized; but we may create service boards or committees directly responsible to those they serve.

10. Alcoholics Anonymous has no opinion on outside issues; hence the A.A. name ought never be drawn into public controversy.

11. Our public relations policy is based on attraction rather than promotion; we need always maintain personal anonymity at the level of press, radio, and films.

12. Anonymity is the spiritual foundation of all our traditions, ever reminding us to place principles before personalities.

More Help from
Messies Anonymous

If you would like more information on Messies Anonymous and information about obtaining the complete Messies Anonymous Super Flipper Kit and other helps including audio/video that are available from Messies Anonymous, visit www.messies.com or write to:

MESSIES ANONYMOUS
5025 Southwest 114th Avenue
Miami, Florida 33165

Sandra Felton's research on the "why" and "how-to" of the problem of messiness continues. She welcomes your comments on this book and any relevant stories from your life which relate to your struggle with the house, whether successful or not.

You can sign up to receive a free, daily coaching email from The Organizer Lady ™ on the messies.com website. Sandra Felton writes these emails to encourage and inspire you to continue to move forward in creating a harmonious and beautiful home.

More books by Sandra Felton

The Messies Manual

The flagship book of M.A. will help you organize activities, pay bills on time, keep a clean house, and more.

Organizing for Life

Declutter your mind to declutter your world

Organizing Magic

Practical ideas to make your life easier and more productive in just 40 days

Living Organized

Makes housekeeping easier and less overwhelming for the organizationally challenged

Smart Organizing

Consolidate, condense, containerize, keep clutter at bay

Meditations for Messies

I've Got to Get Rid of This Stuff

A self-help program designed to make a significant difference in three weeks time.

Organizing Your Home & Family

When You Live with a Messie

Printed in the United States
204963BV00003B/1-39/A

9 780970 862907